Missouri Courthouses:
BUILDING MEMORIES ON THE SQUARE

Sponsored by Missouri Preservation

Missouri Alliance for Historic Preservation (Missouri Preservation) is proud to participate in the publication of *Missouri Courthouses: Building Memories on the Square*. Historically, courthouses have played a vital role in the development of communities across the state and they continue to be repositories of county and state history. Our courthouses can, and should, continue their job of contributing to the livelihood of Missouri's communities and counties in the future.

In 2005, Missouri Preservation placed the historic courthouses of Missouri, as a group, on its list of Most Endangered Historic Places. Many of the state's courthouses are deteriorating due to deferred maintenance, lack of funding, and a lack of understanding of historic preservation methods. We hope that this book will bring public awareness to the plight of the historic courthouse. Hopefully, it will inspire citizens to learn about programs and funds to rehabilitate these significant structures. Adaptive use, or finding new uses for existing buildings, may also help these architectural treasures continue to play an important role in Missouri history.

Missouri Preservation would like to give special thanks to Governor Roger Wilson, for his support, and to Pat Eng and Eng and Woods, attorneys at law, Columbia, Missouri, for their support and sponsorship of this project. Additional gratitude is also extended to Bruce Wilson, Columbia, Missouri, and Boone County Sheriff Dwayne Carey. Thank you to the many volunteers and supporters who recognize the merit of this special project.

Proceeds for this project will benefit Missouri Preservation, a statewide non-profit organization dedicated to saving the irreplaceable historic resources in Missouri. For more information on Missouri Preservation, visit our website at www.preservemo.org.

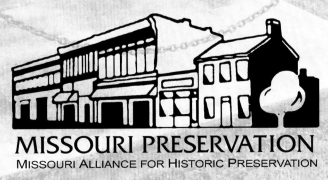

MISSOURI PRESERVATION
MISSOURI ALLIANCE FOR HISTORIC PRESERVATION

Missouri Courthouses:

BUILDING MEMORIES ON THE SQUARE

By Dennis Weiser

THE
DONNING COMPANY
PUBLISHERS

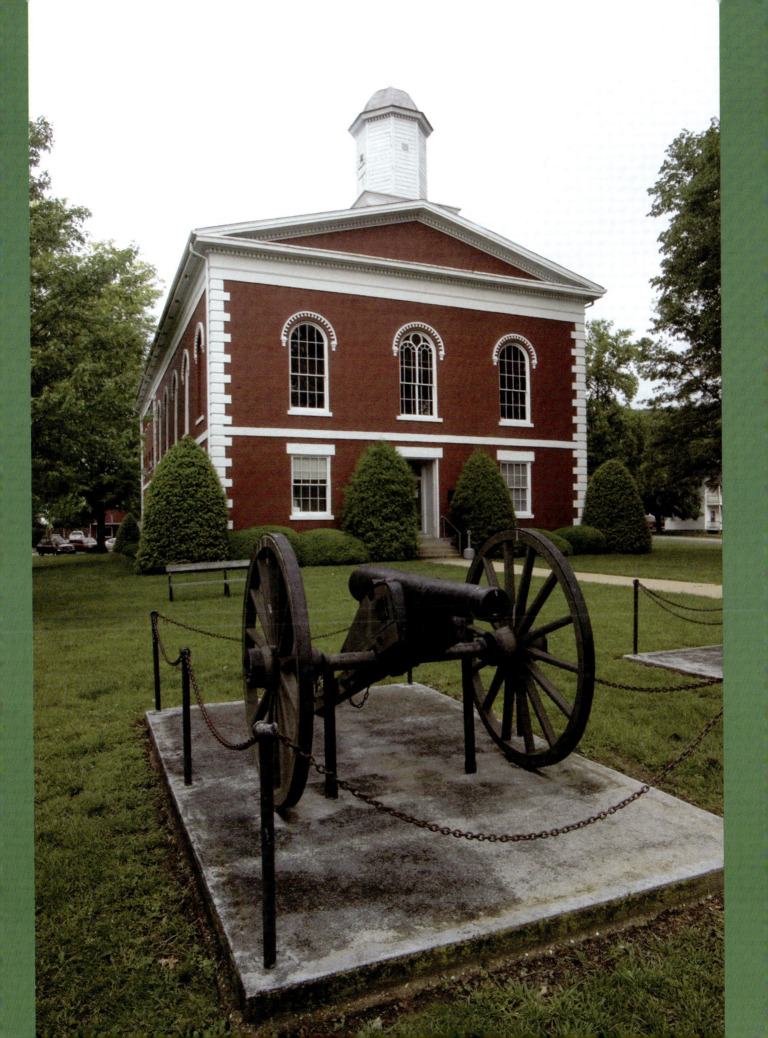

The Donning Company Publishers
184 Business Park Drive, Suite 206
Virginia Beach, VA 23462–6533

Steve Mull, General Manager
Barbara Buchanan, Office Manager
Jamie R. Watson and Ashley Campbell, Editors
Amanda Guilmain, Graphic Designer
Mellanie Denny, Imaging Artist
Scott Rule, Director of Marketing
Cindy Smith, Project Research Coordinator

Ed Williams, Project Director

Library of Congress Cataloging-in-Publication Data
Weiser, Dennis.
   Missouri courthouses : building memories / by Dennis Weiser.
      p. cm.
   Includes bibliographical references and index.
   ISBN-13: 978-1-57864-399-8 (hardcover : alk. paper)
   ISBN-10: 1-57864-399-6 (hardcover : alk. paper)
   1. Courthouses—Missouri. 2. Public architecture—Missouri. I. Title.
   NA4472.M8W45 2006
   725.1509778—dc22
                              2006035570

Printed in the United States of America by Walsworth Publishing Company

Foreword

Dear Friends,

The great state of Missouri is blessed with a grand assortment of cultural achievements, extraordinary events, and memorable architecture. The county courthouses built by our forbearers are visible reminders of the will and desire of our citizens that all who live in Missouri should have the right to choose who will govern, that no one is above the rule of law, and that we share a commitment to justice.

Built on the foundation of democracy, these buildings provide quiet narration of our state's triumphs and tragedies, juries and justice. Standing as monuments, they stir our memories; serving as the home of county government, they protect the future.

In *Missouri Courthouses: Building Memories on the Square,* author Dennis Weiser has assembled a wonderful collection of stories through a series of photographs and facts that celebrate the importance of the courthouse—individually and collectively. This volume is a fine addition to our architectural record of historic buildings and will be a historical reference and guide for future generations of Missourians.

I am pleased Missouri Preservation is sponsoring *Missouri Courthouses: Building Memories on the Square.* As the only statewide, non-profit organization dedicated to promoting historic preservation throughout the Show-Me state, they play an important role in safeguarding places of notable significance to our past.

All of our courthouses are important to each of us as citizens, but one is of particular significance to me both personally and professionally. In 1976, I was elected to the office of Boone County Collector, a post my father, Roger Woodrow Wilson, held before me. My maternal grandfather, Ned Gibbs, served as Boone County Recorder of Deeds. My paternal grandfather, Roger Isaac Wilson, was Boone County Sheriff. In 1933, he was killed in the line of duty, and following his death, his body lay in state in the courthouse where I began my career in public service.

As lieutenant governor and governor, I had the distinct pleasure to visit almost every courthouse in Missouri. Each was unique, but they have a common bond—the county governments and courts these buildings shelter serve us by uniting society while preserving individual freedoms. Through *Missouri Courthouses: Building Memories on the Square,* I hope you enjoy learning about the relevance each courthouse has in Missouri's proud history and tradition.

Sincerely,

Roger Wilson

Contents

Preface

This volume is a pictorial record of Missouri's current 114 county courthouses, including some of the earlier buildings that housed the county governments (the average county in Missouri is now utilizing its third courthouse building). And, while design modification to a particular building may be minor, all but the newest of the existing courthouses have been remodeled and modernized to some degree since they were originally constructed.

The title of "architect" herein is used in a generic sense to identify those individuals who designed the buildings featured in this volume. Nineteenth-century architects learned their trade in a variety of ways, including working as carpenters and draftsmen or studying as apprentices under the supervision of an established architect or firm. Formal academic training for the profession did not begin until 1913, when the University of Kansas first offered architecture course work. In 1942, a law was passed in Missouri requiring professional registration of architects, and the first certification exams were offered in 1944.

I appreciate the cooperation, patience, and goodwill of the elected officials, administrators, staff members, judges, deputies, and law enforcement officers that I met while working on this project. Thank you for responding to my questions and requests with professionalism and courtesy.

My sincere appreciation also goes to the county historic societies that I visited during my travels. Thank you for access to your collections and for allowing display information and artifacts to be included in this volume.

I am grateful for the excellent assistance provided by the state archives personnel at the James Kirkpatrick Center in Jefferson City. I am indebted also to the staff of the Local Records Preservation Program and Conservation Laboratory.

I am also appreciative of the Missouri Preservation (Missouri Alliance for Historic Preservation) for their helpful suggestions and guidance with the terminology used in this book.

Thank you, one and all.

Introduction

The courthouse is the home of a county's legal and administrative life. It is the place where couples go for marriage licenses, where one reports for jury duty, where election results are certified, where vendors bid on road and bridge projects, and where individuals pay their property taxes, record land titles, seek justice, and partake in all of the many privileges and responsibilities associated with being a citizen in this great nation.

Accordingly, access to the courthouse by the people of the county has always been a priority. State legislators emphasized accessibility when they approved the location of county seats as near as possible to the geographic center of each county. The goal when counties were being formed during the nineteenth century was to position a county seat so that a citizen would be able to travel to the courthouse and be home again before sunset, a distance estimated to be about twenty miles.

Some of those county seat communities did not exist prior to the creation of the new county, and a clearing in the wilderness had to be carved out of the backwoods so communities could be built from scratch. Those isolated communities then had to be made accessible to surrounding settlements, and early county courts found themselves engrossed with road and bridge construction projects. Maintaining roads and bridges is still a duty of county commissioners and for the same reason—to make the county seat and local government accessible to all people.

With passage of the Americans with Disabilities Act (ADA) in 1990, the concept of courthouse accessibility evolved and began to include elevators, special parking places, and ramps to ensure access for handicapped and elderly persons. The mandate to ensure accessibility was enlarged in 2002 with passage of the Help America Vote Act (HAVA), and voters are being introduced to new types of voting machines to improve accuracy and accessibility during elections.

The ability to improve courthouse accessibility is being frustrated by an equally important mandate to increase building security to thwart terrorism and random violence. High profile trials and emotion-filled courtrooms are particularly vulnerable, and metal detectors, baggage inspection machines, and restricted entries are increasingly common sights in courthouses. Life in a twenty-first-century courthouse is a search to find the correct balance between unfettered accessibility and restricted admission.

Top: New county election equipment eliminates many of the barriers that may have prevented handicapped citizens from voting in the past. Larry Heiberger (right) of Decision One/ES&S briefs Hubert DeLay Jr., Mississippi County Clerk and Election Authority, on the operation of the county's new central vote tabulator.

Bottom: Security checkpoints have become common sights since 9/11 in many courthouses in Missouri. Employees and citizens like the feeling of safety and try not to be offended by the increased surveillance they receive because they are entering a public building. Steve Fueston (left) and Sarah Nagel, Buchanan County deputy sheriffs, use sophisticated equipment, training, and common sense to monitor the hundreds of people who pass their security station every day.

Courthouses are repositories of a county's historical records. A few hours spent perusing files in a county storage vault might turn up an 1857 list of bounties paid for wolf scalps, a teacher's 1921 student progress report, a blueprint used for a 1930s Public Works Administration road-building project, or the minutes from an 1837 county commissioners' meeting. One antebellum record still on file at the Ste. Genevieve County Courthouse is a list of free persons of color, a disquieting reminder of Missouri's days as a slave state.

Along with maintaining property and legal records, many courthouses are supplementing their written files with richly detailed murals that illustrate major events of the county's history. Courthouses in Pettis, Callaway, Jasper, Howard, Gasconade, Newton, and Clay Counties display such murals. Billboard-sized murals can also be found on buildings located near courthouses in Howell and Cape Girardeau Counties. Murals with patriotic themes and illustrations of local historical features, such as the route of the Wire Telegraph Road and predecessor courthouse buildings, can be found at several other courthouses around the state.

County historical societies also maintain displays in courthouses or in nearby museums. Moniteau County, for example, exhibits Native American artifacts; Jasper County has a collection of Civil War weapons and paraphernalia; and Bollinger County's historical society maintains an authentic log house on the courthouse square. The societies in Pulaski, Johnson, and Phelps Counties preserve entire courthouses from earlier eras as period museums. These volunteer organizations are the heartbeat of historic preservation at the county level.

Courthouses do more than serve as the home for the county's legal and administrative services, provide citizens an accessible place to pay taxes, and store the county's accumulation of local history. They, as Governor Wilson notes in his foreword, represent history and tradition; they represent collective ideals and individual interests. These intangibles are communicated, in part, through their courthouse's architecture via stonework, columns, and monumental entrances. The community's collective identity is reflected in architectural references to classical Greece, Art Deco, or the eclectic ornamentation popular in the late nineteenth century. Missouri's courthouses—many of which are the work of well-known local architects, contractors using pattern book designs, or builders from across the Midwest—are a varied and rich collection of architectural design.

Courthouses tend to be a community's most impressive public building, one that often anchors an important space in the heart of the county seat. They contribute to the sense of

One of the conditions of the Missouri Compromise was that free persons of color would be allowed to reside in the state after being emancipated. This 1856 roster is a list of freed slaves residing in Ste. Genevieve County.

place that makes our state unique, and they are important examples of various traditions within the construction trade and architect profession. Courthouses record the style and construc-

tion techniques of the era in which they were built yet stand to represent a county's identity for generations. One architectural historian, Spiro Kostof, described courthouses as the "monumental gestures that commemorate heroes and mark the passage of our history." Kostof felt that it was at the courthouse where "the prevalent values and beliefs of the community were made manifest."

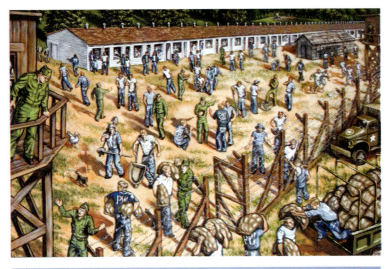

Our courthouses are valuable to Missouri's communities and citizens for these and many more reasons. They deserve to be protected and to be used—if not for their original purposes, than for new functions made possible through creative thinking on the part of their communities. Through historic preservation—the safeguarding and use of historic architecture—courthouses can continue to play a role in the lives of Missourians. Our state's historic courthouses are resources that represent not only the past but Missouri's collective future as well.

Top: The POW panel is part of the multi-panel mural in the Clay Courthouse building. During World War II, German soldiers were held as prisoners-of-war in a camp near Liberty. (From: Clay County Collection. Artist: David McClain, 2000)

Bottom: Johnson County's restored, foursquare courthouse is the only remaining example of one of Missouri's most popular courthouse architectural styles. After 1871, the courthouse was used as a school, church, and private residence until 1965, when it was purchased by the county historical society.

Left: The 1897 Adair County Courthouse was built with modern conveniences such as indoor plumbing, electric lights, and steam heat.

Inset: The courthouse tower was removed during the twentieth century. Today, preservation professionals would choose to preserve the tower, if possible, in order to maintain the original design of the building.

Bottom left: Mary Vogt McIntosh, a field archivist with the Missouri State Archives Local Records Division, is dwarfed by the massive support arches that once supported the tower. The iron brace was affixed to the brickwork in order to stabilize the structure.

Bottom middle: Statues of Justice are commonly used to represent the moral force that underlies the legal system. Justice is not blind, but some iconography shows her wearing a blindfold to indicate that justice is meted out without bias or favoritism.

Bottom right: Jim Lymer, county clerk, inspects an 1867 record of bounties paid to hunters by the county for killing wolves. Wolf packs were a threat to livestock, and by 1900, the wolf population in Missouri was decimated.

Adair County

Organized: January 29, 1841 | County Seat: Kirksville | Architect: Robert G. Kirsch

A schoolhouse, located a few miles south of Kirksville, also served as the home for the Adair County Court until 1843. The court moved to a one-story building located across from the town square on a temporary basis later that year.

In 1853, the county commissioners constructed a foursquare courthouse on the square. Twelve years later, in 1865, this building was destroyed by fire. County officers found shelter in available nooks and crannies around the square, and Adair County's citizens waited thirty years before building their next courthouse.

Voters authorized the third and present courthouse in 1897. The building's ornate architectural style was fashionable during the latter half of the nineteenth century. Adair's courthouse included state-of-the-art infrastructure enhancements such as electric lights, steam heat, and indoor plumbing—modern upgrades for the age.

The 109-year-old building retains much of its original design, but the impressive clock tower proved to be too weighty for its support arches. Twentieth-century restoration work revealed that the tower support bowed under the pressure. Workers removed the central tower during the twentieth century after a brace failed to stabilize the brick arches.

The statue of Justice that once stood upon the highest point of the tower was preserved and has a new place on the roof. The courthouse is listed on the National Register of Historic Places.

Andrew County

Organized: January 29, 1841 | County Seat: Savannah | Architect: George McDonald

During the last 165 years, Andrew County has built three courthouses.

The first was constructed in 1841; it lacked proper accommodations, and the county officials abandoned it after only three years. The second, 1845–98, was a spacious, two-story, brick building surmounted by a tall cupola. This structure was torn down after fifty years of use to make way for the current courthouse. The present courthouse was completed in 1899.

The building was constructed of pressed brick (so called because the brick clay is placed under pressure to eliminate irregularities before being hardened by firing in a kiln). The building is accented with stone at the base, entrance archways, and window openings.

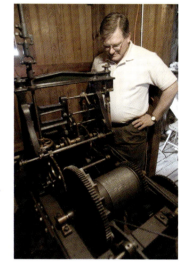

The building's tower clock, manufactured by the Seth Thomas Company, can be seen throughout the square from its place on the tower fifty feet above the roofline. A heroic statue of Liberty continues to adorn the tip of the tower structure, but the four full-size statues of Justice that once stood atop the four corner towers have been removed.

The building was added to the National Register of Historic Places in 1980.

Top left: In 1941, the county observed its centennial with a three-day-long celebration. The program listed activities such as tug of war, a ladies' nail driving contest, sack races, and a checkers tournament.

Top right: Daniel Hegeman, county clerk, admires the mechanics of the courthouse's one-hundred-year-old Seth Thomas clock. An electric motor spools the wire rope to lift the clock's hammer. On the hour, the hammer strikes a stationary bell to toll the time of day. The three-foot-diameter bell and hammer apparatus are located on the floor beneath the clock works. The vertical universal joint (top left) powers horizontal metal rods that turn the hands on each of the tower's clock faces.

Bottom left: The two-story, 1844–99 Andrew County Courthouse was designed by Samuel Knight. (From: Andrew County Collection. Artist: Paul Stock)

Bottom right: A yellow barricade near the main entrance marks the spot where workers are installing an elevator in the 109-year-old building. The Americans with Disabilities Act requires that every citizen must have adequate access to public buildings.

Atchison County

Organized: February 14, 1845 | County Seat: Rock Port | Architects: Edmund J. Eckel and George R. Mann

In 1849, the U.S. Supreme Court resolved a boundary dispute between Missouri and Iowa by awarding the northernmost ten miles of Atchison County to Iowa. This shifting of the state's border caused the town of Linden to lose its position as the Atchison County seat. The prize was given to Rock Port, and Linden's residents complained bitterly and perhaps rightly so, because Rock Port's location was only a few miles farther south—a difference that was hardly discernable on a map. Despite objections from the Linden residents, in 1856 Atchison County officials ordered the sale of the Linden courthouse and further argument was silenced.

Rock Port built a replacement courthouse that same year. That building was home to the county court until the early 1880s, when it was condemned to make way for its replacement. Competition for the honor of being named as the county seat surfaced in 1882. Tarkio, an up-and-coming community, offered to build a new courthouse at no expense to the county as an inducement to be named county seat, but their bid was beaten back.

Perhaps disgruntled by the loss of a free courthouse, Atchison County's voters promptly defeated a forty thousand dollar bond issue that was needed in order to build the courthouse design that had been selected by the county officials. The county commissioners, thwarted by the electorate but still in control of the purse strings, reacted by transferring fifteen thousand dollars from the general revenues account and securing another ten thousand dollars through private subscriptions. These funds were used to begin the construction project on schedule. Thus, the shell of the new courthouse was built, and the interior rooms were finished and furnished over time as the funds became available.

Left: The 1882 Atchison County Courthouse was built on a hill that overlooks the community of Rock Port.

Middle: The clock tower's pyramidal cap has been removed, and the slate on the mansard roof has been replaced with metal sheeting. (Courtesy: Atchison County, photo montage of 1903–04 county officers)

Bottom: Deanna Beck, deputy clerk, demonstrates the difficulty of trying to fit a twenty-first-century ballot into an antique ballot box. The cylindrical container was used in early elections and manufactured by the George Barnard Company.

Audrain County

Organized: December 17, 1836 | County Seat: Mexico | Architects: Bonsack and Pearce

Audrain County Court House, Mexico, Missouri

Top: The original design for the 1951 Audrain County Courthouse called for a round tower on the roof and columned porticos at the entrances, but those costly elements were eliminated to keep construction costs within the limits set by the voters.

Top right: The building's three-story, open entrance hall is a design element that pleasantly surprises first-time visitors. A tower above the atrium area was part of the original design but never built. A skylight brightens the vestibule.

Bottom right: The 1868–1949 Audrain County Courthouse was similar in design to a courthouse that was constructed in neighboring Monroe County in 1867.

Rolling prairie land, situated a convenient distance north of the Missouri River and one hundred miles west of the mighty Mississippi, beckoned to settlers who were eager to farm open spaces. Audrain County was formed and Mexico, the county seat, was named in honor of the widespread excitement Missourians were experiencing for Texas, then a republic fighting for its independence from Mexico.

Audrain County's first court met in 1837 in a one-story, hand-hewn log building erected as a temporary courthouse. In November 1840, the court moved to a two-story, brick building located at the center of the square. The county sold the sturdy log building, and it continued its useful life into the 1880s as a bakery and confectionery.

During the Civil War, troops commandeered the courthouse as a barracks, and the building was damaged beyond repair. In 1868, work began on a new courthouse that had ten rooms, with the courtroom on the second floor and a round tower atop the roof.

During the 1930s, many of Missouri's counties took advantage of grants offered by the federal Work Projects Administration (WPA) to build new courthouses. Audrain County proved to be an exception, however, when officials decided not to participate in the federal program after listening to a proposal from a WPA engineer in 1938.

In 1947, the county decided the time was right to replace its aged courthouse and placed a bond issue on the ballot. The county residents voted to approve the obligation, but bids exceeded the five hundred thousand dollar amount appropriated by the voters, and court officials and architects had to adjust the plans to reduce costs. Work began in May 1950 and was finished in the fall of 1951.

Barry County

Organized: January 5, 1835 |
County Seat: Cassville | Architect:
Henry H. Hohenschild

In 1835, the newly formed
county's boundaries stretched
much farther than they do now.
The original Barry County, created
by the state legislature in 1834,
contained the present counties of
Barry, Lawrence, Dade, McDonald,
Newton, Jasper, Barton, and a part
of Cedar County.

Barry's first county seat was at
the town of Mount Pleasant, located on Clear Creek just to the west of present-day Pierce City.
In 1845, when the legislature created Lawrence County, Mount Pleasant was no longer at the
geographic center of Barry County, and Cassville became the new county seat.

The William Kerr farmhouse was the site of early court sessions in Cassville. In 1847, soon
after the move, the court built its first courthouse in Cassville—probably a two-story, wood
building.

The county's next courthouse, constructed in 1855, was the site where Missouri's secession-
ist government met in 1861 to elect delegates to the Congress of the Confederate States. Led by
Missouri's pro-southern governor, Claiborne Fox Jackson, the provisional government voted to
secede from the Union and the Confederacy declared Missouri as its twelfth state, even though
it was under the control of Union troops throughout the war.

Federal troops occupied the courthouse during the Civil War. Troop takeovers were
frequent occurrences during the war because courthouses tended to be large, sturdy buildings
centrally located in a community. With local government suspended during the conflict, the
buildings made convenient troop quarters, hospitals, arsenals, or stables.

The antebellum courthouse was condemned in 1907 and razed in 1910. County business
was carried out at temporary quarters spotted here and there around the square until a new
courthouse could be constructed.

The twentieth-century design of the current courthouse reflected the new attitude toward
architecture that was capturing the imagination of the public. The 1913 building's design—
smooth stones, flat roof, clean lines—was a shift away from the cupolas, towers, and great stone
arches that had entranced Missourians only a generation before.

After ninety years, this courthouse continues to serve the community.

Top: The Barry County Courthouse cost almost
forty-six thousand dollars to build in 1913.
In the last few years, the building has been
renovated with a state-of-the-art, ground-source
heating and air-conditioning system and new
windows.

Bottom: Cherry Warren, presiding county
commissioner, researches state statutes for an
answer to a question concerning county roads.
The jury chairs and judge's bench indicate
the commission's chamber was formerly used
as courtroom. The county's judicial business
is now conducted in a separate facility that
opened in 2003.

Barton County

Organized: December 12, 1855 | County Seat: Lamar | Architect: W. R. Parsons and Sons

Top: The main entry of the Barton County Courthouse features massive, cast-iron supports made locally at the Lamar Iron Works. Harry S. Truman's family lived briefly in Lamar, where the 33rd President of the United States was born.

Top right: The building's original roofline included a central tower and parapets on the corner towers. During the twentieth century, the center tower was removed, and the parapets were replaced with pyramidal roofs. (Courtesy: Barton County Collection)

Bottom right: The spiral staircase, part of the original 1888 construction, was incorporated into a 1976 renovation. Kathleen Dimond, recorder of deeds, descents the 118-year-old metal steps for quick access from the floor above to her office.

Civil War action in 1862 destroyed Barton County's first permanent courthouse. A modest 34-by-20-foot building—two stories high with a weatherboard exterior—became what was to be a temporary courthouse in 1866; nevertheless, it went on to serve as the seat of justice for the next twenty-two years.

In 1888, the court erected the current courthouse. The contractor used local stone and red brick to dress the 80-by-120-foot building. During a twentieth-century renovation, the central tower was removed and the corner tower parapets were replaced with pyramidal roofs. With the exception of those roof alterations, the building looks much as it did in the 1880s.

Bates County

Organized: January 29, 1841 | County Seat: Butler | Architect: George McDonald

In 1821, the United Foreign Missionary Society, a religious organization supported by the Presbyterian, Reformed Dutch, and Associated Reformed churches, established Harmony Mission, the first village in what was to become Bates County. The purpose of the settlement was to introduce the English language and customs to the members of the local Osage tribe so the Native Americans could assimilate more easily with white settlers moving into the area.

In 1841, the Bates County commissioners selected Harmony Mission as the first county seat when Bates was separated from Cass County. Harmony was selected because it was an already functioning community and centrally located in the new county. Nevertheless, in 1847, Papinville, a town three miles southeast of Harmony Mission, became the new county seat. The county's first courthouse was built there in 1855.

That same year, the legislature separated Vernon from Bates County, and Papinville lost its central geographical position. Accordingly, in 1856, the county seat moved once again, this time to Butler, where the county built another courthouse. The Butler building burned in 1861—a consequence of Civil War violence.

The Civil War's disruption of the county government necessitated the relocation of the court and administrative services to several different communities during the conflict. In 1864, the court met at Johnstown, and the next year, Pleasant Gap became the county seat. After the Civil War, citizens rebuilt the devastated town of Butler and patched together a temporary courthouse and county clerk's office. Those buildings sufficed for about four years.

In 1869, with Reconstruction well underway, county officials built a three-story courthouse. The court selected a design that featured the Second Empire style, and that handsome building served for thirty years before being declared unsafe in 1899. The present courthouse became home to county officials in 1902.

Top: The 1901 Bates County Courthouse design was based on the same plan used to build the Andrew, Johnson, and Lawrence County Courthouses.

Inset: The statue of Liberty was removed from the tower sometime in the twentieth century and reinstalled during the summer of 2006. The ornate and colorful decorations under the eves of the corner towers add visual interest.

Bottom: Bates County's first county seat was at Harmony Mission. The mission was located close to the Osage River near the southern border of present-day Bates County. When Vernon County was created in 1855, the Bates county seat was moved to Butler. (From: Missouri State Capitol. Lunette by William Knox)

Benton County

Organized: January 3, 1835 | County Seat: Warsaw | Architect: George A. Masters

In 1838, after meeting for several years at various farmhouses around the county, the court ordered the construction of a hewn-log building to serve as a temporary courthouse. Four years later, the county replaced the log structure with the first permanent courthouse. This building served the county for the next thirty-nine years until it was condemned when workmen discovered the foundation was in danger of collapsing and the court ordered work to begin on a replacement courthouse.

Construction of the current courthouse was split between two contractors and occurred in stages. In December 1886, the first contractor completed the shell of the building, which consisted of the foundation, walls, and roof. A different contractor finished the interior work in mid-1887.

During the 1930s, a Work Projects Administration grant was used to install a fishpond at the rear of the building. The area now is used as a flower garden.

In 1974, a new entry was installed, and it dramatically altered the appearance of the building. The 120-year-old building continues to serve Benton County.

Top: Children pose beside the county courthouse's WPA fishpond. (From: Postcard, Carla Brown collection)

Bottom left: Rodney Meyer, presiding commissioner, answers a constituent's question sent to him via the county's e-mail system.

Bottom right: The main entrance of the nineteenth-century Benton County Courthouse was redesigned in 1974. The building was originally constructed in 1886–87 and cost $9,089.

Bollinger County

Organized: March 1, 1851 | County Seat: Marble Hill | Architect: Morris Frederick Bell

Bollinger County's boundaries were redrawn several times. Before becoming an independent county in 1851, Bollinger was part of Wayne, Cape Girardeau, and Stoddard counties. When the legislature established Bollinger County, the county commissioners decided to name the new county seat Dallas, but they later changed the name of the town to Marble Hill.

In 1852, the county officials constructed their first courthouse, a 30-foot-square, brick, two-story building. That foursquare courthouse was consumed by fire in 1866.

A wood frame building, similar in size and configuration to the earlier courthouse, followed in 1867. Seventeen years later, that building was condemned, and after it was abandoned, it was destroyed by fire.

The current courthouse was built in 1885. Originally a 50-by-60-foot building, the courthouse was enlarged with an addition in 1912, and more renovation followed in the 1960s and '70s.

Top: Rose Ann Thiele, a volunteer with the Bollinger County Historical Society, leads tours through the restored 1869 Massey House located on the county courthouse square. Members of the historical society maintain the county's historic records and assist with genealogy research.

Bottom: The 1885 Bollinger County Courthouse was enlarged in 1912. The building's octagonal cupola with a square base was removed sometime in the twentieth century.

Boone County

Organized: November 16, 1820 | County Seat: Columbia | Architect: J. H. Felt.

Legal informalities such as open-air trials were common in nineteenth-century Missouri, when pleasant weather made outdoor sessions agreeable. When rain threatened, a nearby farmhouse, church, or pub would serve as well.

The niceties of civilization advanced quickly on the frontier, however, and in 1824, the court built its first courthouse in Boone County. It was a foursquare, brick, two-story building. Court met on the first floor and county offices were located on the second story. By 1845, the building was worn and ready for replacement.

The second courthouse was completed in 1847 and faced south. The building's four portico columns aligned with the portico columns on the north-facing Academic Hall (built in 1841) at the University of Missouri. George Caleb Bingham, artist and state treasurer during the Civil War, maintained a studio in this courthouse.

The old courthouse was razed and the university's Academic Hall burned during the intervening years, but the columns—all that are left of the two buildings—still stand in alignment.

Work on the current courthouse began in 1906. The original building specifications called for a taller, rounded cupola structure, but this met with disapproval, and the dome was built much closer to the roofline.

Top: Staff and duties have grown with the county's expansion over the years, and the 1906 Boone County Courthouse is now used exclusively for court business. Many of the county's administrative offices are housed at the Boone County Government Center, an annex located on the square immediately east of the courthouse.

Middle: The columns of the university's administration building that burned in 1894 align with the Boone County Courthouse columns. The 1847 courthouse, still standing in this postcard photograph, was razed in 1909. (From: Library of Congress)

Bottom left: This depiction of frontier law shows a lawyer arguing his case before a jury during an open-air circuit court trial held in Boone County. Such trials were common, but participants sought cover when the weather turned for the worst. (From: Missouri State Capitol. Lunette by Walter Ufer)

Bottom right: George Caleb Bingham moved to Columbia to secure portrait commissions and maintained a studio near the law office of his friend and sponsor James Sidney Rollins, the father of the University of Missouri. Several of Bingham's famous politically themed paintings include the 1847-1909 Boone County Courthouse. (From: Columbia Guitar building. Murals by Sidney Larson, 1989)

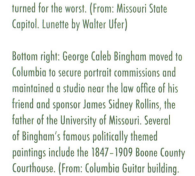

THE FIRST CIRCUIT COURT IN BOONE COUNTY

Buchanan county

Organized: December 31, 1838 | County Seat: St. Joseph | Architect: P. F. Meagher

In 1839, Buchanan County court sessions were held at a newly created town called Benton, later renamed Sparta. A two-room, log building served as the first courthouse.

In 1846, citizens voted to move the county seat to St. Joseph, an example of one of the few times when a county seat is not located at the geographic center of a county. Joseph Robidoux, the founder of St. Joseph, donated land for the courthouse square. Robidoux, a pioneer entrepreneur, built his fortune trading with the Native Americans, primarily in the Platte Territory. When the international fur trade collapsed, the astute merchant switched his business interests from trading beaver pelts to land speculation and supplying goods to the American settlers coming into the territory.

The county court built the 1847 courthouse on a hillside with a commanding view over the young community. The classical-revival-style building featured an impressive cupola that capped the 50-by-75-foot, two-story building. The courthouse deteriorated with age, however, and county officials vacated it in 1871.

In 1873, the county court authorized construction of the present courthouse. St. Joseph was enjoying its golden era as a shipping and transportation hub in the 1870s, and grandeur seemed appropriate. The architect designed a somewhat unusual layout, roughly in the shape of a Greek cross, and gave the building three porticoes that face east, west, and south. A splendid dome, forty feet in diameter, soared sixty feet above the roofline. Observation parapets provided views of the entire town. Sadly, a fire gutted the building in 1885, and the dome was reconfigured during the rebuilding.

In 1979, the building was restored, and the original red brick surface was revealed after having been covered by white paint for many years. The interior space was expanded, but only the east entrance remains in use today due to security restrictions. The courthouse is listed on the National Register of Historic Places.

Butler County

Organized: February 27, 1849 | County Seat: Poplar Bluff | Architect: N. S. Spencer and Sons

In 1849, surveyors platted the town of Poplar Bluff as the county seat. The county officials had selected a site on an uninhabited bluff on the Black River and named it for the profusion of poplar trees growing in the area. Within a year, the new town attracted ten families and grew steadily over the years.

Opposite page

Top: Bud Crockett, 81, Buchanan County's Western District Commissioner, tries to spend several hours at the courthouse each day and is proud of his sixteen years of service as county commissioner.

Middle: The busy main lobby of the Buchanan County Courthouse receives natural lighting from the dome skylight and features twin grand staircases from the 1870s.

Bottom: The dome on the 1873 Buchanan County Courthouse was destroyed by fire in 1885 and replaced with an attractive, but slightly less prominent, structure.

This page

Top: The 1927 Butler County Courthouse design is an example of the classical revival style that was in favor after the turn of the twentieth century.

Bottom: Marion L. Tibbs, the Butler County Assessor, commissioned a mural depicting the county's three courthouses for the wall outside his office. (Butler County Collection. Artist: Bradley Wilson, 2005)

The county authorized the sale of ten thousand acres of swampland in 1858 to pay for a courthouse building, but the project failed to generate sufficient revenue. The venture was undermined by the devastation caused by the Civil War and possible fraudulent activities connected with the land sales. In any case, in 1866 the court tried anew and was more successful. The contract was awarded to new builders, and a foursquare, brick courthouse was completed in 1867. This building burned in 1886.

A replacement courthouse was ready for occupancy in 1887. Unfortunately, in 1927 this courthouse, along with a large swath of Poplar Bluff, was demolished by a tornado that roared through the center of the town. Eighty-seven people died in that violent storm.

In 1928, the community began rebuilding, and the current courthouse rose from the debris and scattered dreams.

Caldwell County

Organized: December 29, 1836 |
County Seat: Kingston | Architect:
L. Grant Middaugh

The town of Far West, the site of the Mormon Church's settlement in Missouri, was Caldwell County's first county seat. A schoolhouse doubled as the first courthouse. After the forced expulsion of the Saints from Missouri in 1838, the Mormons had to abandon Far West, and in 1843 the town of Kingston became the new county seat.

It is unclear if the county officials built a new courthouse in Kingston or moved into an existing building. In either case, the county built a new courthouse in 1847 or 1854, a two-story, brick building that burned in 1860. In 1896, the replacement courthouse also burned.

The series of courthouse fires encouraged the town of Hamilton to vie for the honor of becoming the county seat. However, their petition did not reach the two-thirds voter approval threshold, and Kingston remained the county seat.

In 1898, the court approved construction of the current court-house. The architect's plans called for rounded towers flanking both sides of the south-facing entrance and reaching from the base to the roofline. The towers were renovated in 1994.

The Caldwell County Court-house is listed on the National Register of Historic Places.

Top: An open balcony that overlooks the double entryway connects the twin towers of the 1898 Caldwell County Courthouse. The tower on the right contains a circular staircase.

Middle: The 1860–96 Caldwell County Courthouse was a temple-front building that resembled the 1847 Lafayette County and the 1856 Ray County Courthouses. (From: Caldwell County Collection. Artist: Hazel Martin)

Bottom: Dale Hartley, Caldwell County commissioner, scans a record of the county's 1901–11 railroad tax receipts. Railroad fees and taxes funded schools and other county services. The tower interiors were renovated in 1994.

Callaway County

Organized: November 25, 1820 | County Seat: Fulton | Architects: E. C. Henderson Jr., Paul Elsner, and Clark Merrick

Top right: The 1856 Callaway County Courthouse was a temple front design, but an 1885 remodeling significantly altered the appearance of the building.

Middle: The 1938 Callaway County Courthouse is one of the many Work Projects Administration courthouses that were built in Missouri between 1935 and 1943.

The town of Elizabeth was Callaway County's original county seat. The town no longer exists but is thought to have been located about six miles south of present-day Fulton. In 1825, the county seat was moved to Fulton. Two years later, county officials built a 36-foot-square brick courthouse. This courthouse was razed in 1856 to make way for its replacement.

In 1856, the county constructed a classic-style building. The portico over the front entrance featured six columns instead of the customary four, and a large tower crowned the roofline. In 1885, the building was remodeled with the addition of a dome and a mansard roof. The renovation blended several architectural styles, which was typical for this period, but it was demolished in 1938. The dedication plaque from the 1856 courthouse is preserved on a second-story corridor wall in the present Callaway County courthouse.

In June 1938, voters approved a bond issue for a new courthouse. Passage of the issue triggered a grant from the Work Projects Administration, and construction began that same year. The project was completed in December 1939, and dedication of the building took place March 18, 1940.

Bottom left: James Callaway, grandson of Daniel Boone, was a hero of the War of 1812. He was killed in March 1815 by Native Americans in what has been called the last battle of that war. (From: Missouri State Capitol. Lunette by Bert G. Phillips)

Bottom right: Lee Fritz, presiding commissioner, pauses near a plaque from the 1856 courthouse. Public buildings customarily list the names of county officials, building committee members, architects, construction supervisors, and contractors associated with the project. This roster also includes the name of the stonecutter, J. Staub.

Camden County

Organized: January 29, 1841 | County Seat: Camdenton | Architect: Victor DeFoe

Camden County was originally named Kinderhook, for President Martin Van Buren's estate or perhaps the president's nickname of "Old Kinderhook." In 1843, the Missouri state legislators voted to change the name to Camden in honor of Charles Pratt, First Earl of Camden, an advocate of civil liberties and an opponent of taxation on the American colonies without representation.

In 1846, officials ordered construction of a two-story, 40-foot-square, brick courthouse at the town of Erie, located near the Osage River. In 1855, county officials elected to move the county seat to Linn Creek, and the Erie Courthouse was sold at auction. A temporary courthouse was quickly built in Linn Creek.

Following the Civil War, in 1867, county officials decided to proceed with construction of a permanent courthouse in Linn Creek. They used the old Erie Courthouse building design as the model for the new courthouse. In 1902, a fire severely damaged this courthouse and its contents.

After three years, the court agreed to rebuild the courthouse. Contractors joined the still-standing brick walls of the burned-out building with the new construction and managed to double the footprint of the new building without too great of an increase in cost. A rounded cupola capped the roof, and a third-story dormer window provided light for a small jury room.

In 1930, rising waters forced the relocation of the Camden county seat. Bagnell Dam, Union Electric's (now AmerenUE) huge hydroelectric generation project, impounded the Osage River. The Lake of the Ozarks covered old Linn Creek.

The electric company compensated the county for the loss of its old courthouse, and the newly created town of Camdenton became the county seat. In 1932, the courthouse was completed and continues in use today.

Top: The county clerk's office is a linchpin position in the courthouse when it comes to coordinating the county's activities with the many state and federal agencies that share jurisdiction. Rowland Todd, Camden County Clerk (left) speaks frequently with the Missouri secretary of state's office in Jefferson City on election matters that affect Camden County citizens.

Bottom: The Camden County Courthouse has grown to include a judicial services building that was constructed in 1999. The 1931 Camden courthouse is considered the first of the modern-style courthouses to be built in Missouri.

Cape Girardeau County

Organized: October 1, 1812 | County Seat: Jackson | Architect: P. H. Weathers

Before 1812, title to land in the town of Cape Girardeau passed through French and Spanish ownership before being sold to American settlers. Attempts to honor old land grant claims, while also making land available for sale to newly arriving settlers, led to legal actions that took decades to untangle. Such a conflict arose over land that was donated for use as a courthouse square in Cape Girardeau. The court decided that rather than wait an interminable time for a clear title, it would purchase land in the nearby town of Jackson and locate the county seat there.

In 1818, commissioners constructed a plain courthouse that was destroyed by fire in 1837. The replacement courthouse also burned in 1870. The fire-leery commissioners ordered the county's 1872 courthouse to be built without using wood. This sturdy building was demolished, stone by stone, brick by brick, in 1908 to make way for the current courthouse.

Cape Girardeau County is one of the few counties in Missouri with two courthouses. In 1854, the county built a courthouse in the city of Cape Girardeau to hear common pleas (civil actions). The 152-year-old building stands on land that was ceded to the city as a civic center by Louis Lormier, the last Spanish commandant of the Cape Girardeau District of Upper Louisiana (the colonial name for Missouri before the Louisiana Purchase). In addition to the courthouse, Lormier's park has been the scene of many activities over the years—from slave auctions to religious gatherings.

Top: The present courthouse in Jackson was completed in 1908. Most of the county's administrative offices are now housed in the 1987 Cape Girardeau County Administration Building.

Inset: The fleur-de-lis skylight design in the Cape Girardeau County Courthouse in Jackson refers to a time when Missouri was a part of France's colonial territories.

Bottom left: Charles P. Hutson, circuit court clerk for the past thirty-two years, poses with the statue of a Civil War soldier that was part of a memorial at the Court of Common Pleas Courthouse in Cape Girardeau. The statue was damaged and, after being moved to Jackson, replaced by an identical statue.

Bottom right: The Common Pleas Courthouse in Cape Girardeau has been a full-time judicial center since its construction in 1854. The stately building sits on a high bluff overlooking the Mississippi River.

Carroll County

Organized: January 2, 1833 | County Seat: Carrollton | Architect: Robert G. Kirsch

In 1841, the sale of Carroll County's 1835 courthouse produced a $176.50 profit when it sold at auction, probably because the lot was included in the $450 sale price. Construction of the second courthouse progressed slowly. Work began in 1839 on the foursquare building and continued at irregular intervals over the next seventeen years. Carpenters finally added a cupola in 1855, a few years before the building was condemned and razed in 1865.

In 1867, the third courthouse was completed. It was a rectangular, brick, two-story building, somewhat plain in appearance. In 1901, the building was razed to make way for the current courthouse.

The design of the 1904 courthouse compensated for the county's previous conservatively styled buildings. However, while the facade of the courthouse remains unchanged, the central tower and domes from the four corner towers were removed during twentieth-century renovations.

Top: The 1901 Carroll County Courthouse shares the same design that Architect Kirsch used for courthouses in Adair (1897), Polk, and Vernon Counties (1906).

Middle: Carroll County Commissioners Jim Stewart (left), Nelson Heil, and David Martin meet in chambers with the county's bridge foreman, Terry Fry, to discuss personnel assignments. The county commissioners' duties include the construction and repair of the county's roads and bridges. Carroll County has more bridges to maintain than any county of comparable size in Missouri.

Bottom: Early in his long career as a world famous sculptor, Frederick C. Hibbard created the statue of General James Shields that stands at the Carroll County Courthouse. The Shields monument was erected in 1910. Hibbard, born in 1881 at Canton, Missouri, attended Culver-Stockton College before beginning his training as a sculptor in Chicago. His numerous Civil War memorials include a statue of Jefferson Davis at Frankford, Kentucky, and the bronze statue of General U.S. Grant on horseback looking over the battlefield at the Vicksburg National Military Park. His non–Civil War-related creations include the Mark Twain and the Tom Sawyer & Huck Finn monuments at Hannibal, Missouri.

Carter County

Organized: March 10, 1859 | County Seat: Van Buren | Architects (1936): Heckenlively and Mark

Top: This note indicates the government paid $1,900 for the stone and masonry work associated with the restoration of the building. (From: Dennis Boxx collection)

Inset: Betty Ann Ligons, deputy clerk in the circuit court clerk's office, displays a photo of the county's first courthouse, a two-story, hewn-log building that was constructed in 1867.

Bottom: The 1871 Carter County Courthouse was enlarged and remodeled in 1936 with the aid of a Work Projects Administration grant. It is the only courthouse in Missouri with a native fieldstone facade.

In 1859, the state legislature divided Carter from Ripley County. Even though they were no longer in their own county, the Carter County commissioners continued to use the old courthouse for a few years more. It was located about one-half mile west of Van Buren and on the opposite bank of the Current River. In 1867, the commissioners authorized a temporary building in Van Buren and workmen promptly constructed an 18-by-24-foot, hewn-log structure.

The current courthouse replaced the log building in 1871. Originally, the new courthouse was a foursquare, 40-by-40-foot, two-story building. It was built from hand-planed, pine lumber and stood on a rock foundation.

During the 1930s, the building received extensive remodeling. This work, funded by a Work Projects Administration grant, drastically altered the appearance of the building. The county added 2,100 square feet to the original structure. This produced the dimension and silhouette of the present building. Next, the exterior was dressed with native fieldstones. Stone exteriors are common throughout southern Missouri, but the Carter County Courthouse is unique as the only example of such a covering for a Missouri courthouse.

After 135 years, the core structure has been obscured beneath renovations and expansions, but the old courthouse continues to serve the people of Carter County.

Cass County

Organized: March 3, 1835 | County Seat: Harrisonville | Architect: W. C. Root

In 1835, this county was named Van Buren, but the state legislature changed the county's name to Cass in 1849. This tribute, coming on the heels of Cass's unsuccessful presidential race, was probably in recognition of his staunch support of the doctrine of popular sovereignty—the concept that the people living in a territory should be able to determine for themselves whether or not to permit slavery.

When Cass County built its first courthouse remains a question. But, in 1843, a documented courthouse was built on the public square. A replacement courthouse was authorized in 1860, but the public voiced concern over the county's depressed financial condition. Despite the warning flag, county officials decided to proceed with their plans and contracted for the manufacture of three hundred thousand bricks to build a new courthouse. Soon after the bricks were delivered, the outbreak of the Civil War halted the project. After the war, the county sold the unused bricks to repair the damages caused by the conflict to the old courthouse.

In 1897, the county built the current courthouse. The three-story, yellow brick courthouse, with its asymmetrical tower, low-pitched rooflines, and arcading windows, is an example of the Italianate style in architecture.

Top: The 1897 Cass County Courthouse dominates the square in Harrisonville. The building's off-center, open tower is reminiscent of Italian bell towers. This style of architecture was an alternative to the popular Romanesque style of the late nineteenth century.

Bottom: General Thomas Ewing's infamous Order No. 11 decimated Cass County. The order was issued in retaliation for a Rebel attack on Lawrence, Kansas. Missouri artist George Caleb Bingham opposed the eviction order as an atrocity against civilians, and he painted this inflammatory portrait to place blame on General Ewing. After the war, the painting was used by Ewing's opponents to end his political career. (Used by permission, State Historical Society of Missouri, Columbia)

Cedar County

Organized: February 14, 1845 | County Seat: Stockton | Architect: Marshall and Brown

When deciding on what to name the Cedar County seat, the citizens vacillated several times before finally settling on Stockton. In 1846, they called the town Lancaster. In 1847, they changed the name to Fremont to honor John Fremont, the explorer and son-in-law of the powerful Missouri Senator Thomas Hart Benton. The "Great Pathfinder," as Fremont was known, lost his opportunity for Missouri immortality, however, because of his highly publicized, anti-slavery views. He suffered the same loss of political followers as did his famous father-in-law Benton, and the town changed its name from Fremont in 1859 to Stockton. Commodore Robert Stockton was a hero of the Mexican War and was, ironically, the man who helped the then-young Captain Fremont gain national prominence by appointing him as the military governor of California during the Mexican War.

In 1847, the county purchased a house to serve as a temporary courthouse. The county authorized construction of the first permanent courthouse in 1852, and that building was ready for occupancy in the fall of 1855. Only eight years later, however, that courthouse was destroyed by fire during one of the innumerable Civil War scrimmages that plagued Missouri.

In 1867, county officials decided to build anew, and the replacement courthouse was a two-story, brick building with a 46-by-50-foot base. A leaking roof on the new structure was repaired, and this courthouse served the county for the next seventy years.

In 1939, the county began construction on Cedar County's current courthouse. Officials worried about space on the old courthouse square, so the replacement building was built on a new site south of the old square. The builders utilized a new technique to construct this building. Instead of brick or stone, the specifications called for poured concrete. Poured concrete buildings are commonplace today, but Cedar County's courthouse was the first of its type in Missouri when it was dedicated in January 1940.

Top: The 1938 Cedar County Courthouse survived relatively unscathed after a 2003 tornado swept through Stockton and destroyed large sections of the town. The building's monolithic, concrete construction made the courthouse virtually fireproof as well as impervious to high winds.

Bottom: Eddie Johnson, Cedar County Assessor, uses aerial maps to check boundary lines before he makes on-site visits to assess property values for taxation purposes. The assessor inspects property on a constant basis to keep up with the county's two-year assessment cycle.

Chariton County

Organized: November 16, 1820 | County Seat: Keytesville | Architect: Carroll Hutchens

Chariton officials met without a courthouse during the county's first decade. In 1833, James Keyte donated land for public buildings, and Keytesville, a town named in his honor, became the new county seat. The first courthouse was constructed that year. In 1864, a fire during the Civil War destroyed the foursquare building.

A replacement courthouse was built in 1867. The two-story, brick building was topped with a cupola but fire destroyed this courthouse in 1973.

The replacement courthouse is a compromise design. The architect's plan, submitted in 1973, coincided with the court's preference for a modernistic design with a flat roof and horizontal lines. However, some citizens expressed their disappointment when a drawing of the projected building was made public, calling instead for a courthouse with more of the familiar nineteenth-century architectural nuances.

Some new exterior plans were submitted at the request of the court, but the architect left the basic floor plan unchanged. The court selected one of the revised exterior plans, and construction of the building was completed in 1975.

Top: The 1974 Chariton County Courthouse is a composite design that incorporates modern building features with traditional courthouse design elements.

Bottom: The 1867 Chariton County Courthouse was destroyed by fire in 1973. The blaze started while workmen were sandblasting near the building.

Christian County

Organized: March 8, 1859 | County Seat: Ozark | Architect: Henry H. Hohenschild

In 1860, county officials built a two-story, frame courthouse that was destroyed by an arsonist's torch in 1865. The county's second courthouse was ready for occupancy only a year later and served the community for forty-eight years before it was razed.

In 1913, county officials sought to go forward with the sale of bonds to finance a new courthouse, but took the unusual route of neglecting to seek public approval beforehand. New state legislation made this a legal option, and Christian County was the first to try to exercise the opportunity. The citizens of the county did not view the move favorably, however, and political name-calling, World War I–related building restrictions, and threats of legal action bogged down the issue for the next five years.

In 1919, a new court was elected and managed to regain the trust of the voters and, even though saddled with obligations made by the previous court, moved the issue forward. The present courthouse building was completed in 1920.

Politics delayed construction of the 1919 Christian County Courthouse. Animosity was already simmering over a possible change in the location of the county seat and boiled over when the commissioners tried to build a new courthouse without a vote of the people.

Clark County

Organized: December 15, 1818 | County Seat:
Kahoka | Architect: W. B. Larkworthy

Clark County tried three different county seats
before settling on the town of Kahoka. For the first
ten years of its existence, Waterloo was the seat; then,
in 1847, the county seat was moved for seven years to
Alexandria, a town on the banks of the Mississippi,
but flooding prompted a move back to Waterloo. Fortunately, the courthouse in Waterloo was
still available.

Still not satisfied, the court moved the county seat one more time to Kahoka in 1865. The
reasons for this final move are murky, but individuals with vested real estate interests in the
Kahoka area may have been involved in the transaction.

In 1870, construction began on the current courthouse. The 136-year-old brick building is
two stories high with a 45-by-72-foot base. A rounded cupola rises above the roofline. In 1934, a
WPA grant was used to apply stucco to building's exterior walls. An elevator has been added to
the east side of the building. The Clark County building is one of the few remaining examples of
Missouri's 1870s-era courthouses.

Top: The 1870 Clark County Courthouse is
the only courthouse built in Kahoka since the
legislature moved the county seat to that town
in 1865. A separate Law Enforcement Center
annex was built in 1997 on the square.

Bottom: The painting of the Clark County
Courthouse that hangs in the office of Mary D.
Jones, Clerk of the Circuit Court and Ex-officio
Recorder, shows the building as it looked
before stucco was added in 1934. Jones's son
Gary made the painting in 1983 while still in
high school.

Clay County

Organized: January 2, 1822 | County Seat: Liberty | Architect: Wight and Wight

In 1829, county officials ordered construction of the county's first courthouse, but progress was slow and it took until 1833 before the building was completed. The 44-foot-square, brick building burned in 1857.

Construction on a replacement courthouse was started that same year. The building had a circular tower and protruding wings that flanked the primary entrance. This unique-looking building was razed in 1934 in anticipation of the construction of a replacement courthouse.

At the height of the 1930s Depression, President Franklin Roosevelt's administration tried several economic experiments in attempt to instigate a national recovery. Perhaps the best known of these was the Work Projects Administration, an aggressive government agency that used the power of the national treasury to fund local construction projects, especially courthouses. Representatives of the WPA actively lobbied local governments to apply for grants.

In 1934, WPA engineers were successful in stimulating the Clay County commissioners' interest in building a courthouse. The citizens responded with a favorable bond election, and county officials submitted a grant application to the WPA office in Washington. In 1936, the present courthouse was completed.

Top: Started in 1935, the Clay County Courthouse was partially funded by a Work Projects Administration grant and is an outstanding example of a government project completed as scheduled during the darkest days of the Great Depression.

Bottom left: The grand hallway of the courthouse dazzles visitors with its murals, sculpture, and ornate ceiling and wall decorations. Clay County's public buildings are renowned for their displays of public art.

Bottom right: This watercolor shows the covered, two-story porch that stretched across two wings of the 1857–1934 courthouse designed by architect Peter McDuff. (From: Clay County Collection. Artist: Jim Hamil, 1999)

Clinton County

Organized: January 2, 1833 |
County Seat: Plattsburg |
Architect: Reed and Williams

In 1834, Clinton County built a foursquare, two-story, brick courthouse at the county seat, which was named Springfield at the time. The county seat had been named Concord the year before, but citizens decided they liked the name of Springfield instead. However, they soon discovered that a town in Greene County had already laid claim to that name. So in 1835, they were forced to switch their town's name for the final time. They chose Plattsburg.

The 1834 courthouse was replaced in 1860 by a rectangular building fronted by an imposing portico with four large columns. An impressive tower added to the grandeur, but unfortunately this building burned in 1895.

The replacement courthouse literally rose from the ashes by utilizing the still-standing walls of the burned building. Workers removed the tower and changed the entrance design. Changes continued to alter the outward appearance of the building over the next seventy-nine years, until fire destroyed this courthouse for the second time in 1974.

County officials chose to go with a modern design for the current courthouse and occupied the new structure in June 1975.

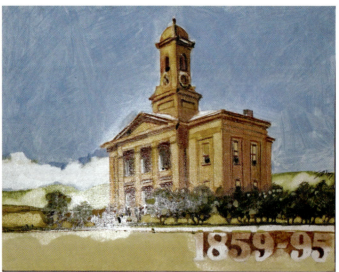

This page

Top: The 1975 Clinton County Courthouse is a postmodern-style building. The low, brick building has multiple roof slopes and is completely devoid of porticos, cupolas, and other building features that are reminiscent of nineteenth-century courthouses.

Bottom left: Molly Livingston, Clinton County circuit clerk and ex-officio recorder of deeds, demonstrates a drum that was ince used for drawing the numbers of prospective jury members.

Bottom right: The 1860–95 Clinton County Courthouse burned, but its fire-blackened walls were incorporated in the construction of the 1895–1974 courthouse building. (Artist: Steve Mayse, 1977)

Opposite page

Top: The ornate, decorative stone carvings on the Cole County Courthouse include this grotesque, a semi-human face surrounded by foliage forms—a traditional image that represents the irrepressible life force of nature merging with humanity.

Middle: The trompe l'oeil balcony scene in the second floor courtroom was added in 1997 as part of a building wide restoration project.

Bottom: The 1896 Cole County Courthouse was built to be "practically fireproof," but a fire in 1918 necessitated a complete restoration of the interior of the building. The architectural style is Romanesque.

Cole County

Organized: November 16, 1820 | County Seat: Jefferson City | Architect: Frank B. Miller

In 1820, the Cole County seat was at Marion, a small town on the Missouri River about ten miles upstream from present-day Jefferson City. Nine years later, the county seat was relocated to Jefferson City, the site of the state capital. Early Cole County courts held their sessions in private homes around the area and occasionally at the state capitol and the old post office.

In 1836, citizens built their first permanent courthouse. This building stood until 1896, even though it had been condemned as unsafe five year earlier. In 1895, voters approved a bond issue for a new courthouse. Officials ordered the old building razed before it collapsed, and services were provided at the present courthouse beginning in 1896.

The first story of the courthouse is stone with pressed brick, and stone trim is used to great effect on the second story. Stone carvings and decorative elements highlight the facade. A fire in 1918 caused serious damage, but the building was restored.

The courthouse interior was again restored in 1997. Tom Sater, a nationally recognized restoration expert, supervised the project

and returned the building's interior to its 1918 condition. When he found the circuit courtroom's balcony area enclosed, with only the original balusters in place, Sater decided to use a deceive-the-eye decorating technique, also known as trompe l'oeil. The missing balcony seats, doorways, and corridor ceiling have been painted on the upper walls of the courtroom, creating an illusion that those features are still in place. The 110-year-old courthouse is listed on the National Register of Historic Places.

Cooper County

Organized: December 17, 1818 | County Seat:
Boonville | Architect: Robert G. Kirsch

Cooper County realized $16, 245 in 1821 from the
sale of public lands put on the market to pay for a new
courthouse and jail. Feeling prosperous, the court
contracted to spend nearly $10,000 for a foursquare
courthouse—an impressive sum for the early 1820s—
and that building was completed in 1823. The fact
that such an expensive building required replacement
after only fifteen years raised eyebrows.

The Cooper County Commission's penchant for
building expensive courthouses continued. In 1838,
the court budgeted $10,800 for its second courthouse,
but ended up spending about $30,000, also a dispro-
portionately large amount for a public building of that
era. That courthouse served for seventy-four years, however. Plans for a replacement were laid
before the community in 1911.

In 1912, the community observed the cornerstone celebration for the present courthouse.
The county accepted the new building from the contractor in 1913.

Top: The Cooper County Courthouse helped
convince other counties that the time had
come to move away from the towers, arches,
and heavy stonework that characterized the
previous generation of architectural design.

Bottom: Darryl Kempf, Cooper County Clerk,
points to restoration work that returned the
courthouse interior to its original color scheme.
The elevator behind Kempf was installed
in 2003 to comply with the Americans with
Disabilities Act.

Crawford County

Organized: January 23, 1829 | County Seat: Steelville | Architect: J. J. Upchurch

In 1829, Crawford County's original boundaries included most of Phelps County and part of Dent County. The county seat was located on the Little Piney River, a stream that begins its flow south of present-day Rolla and continues into the Mark Twain National Forest in southwestern Phelps County.

In 1835, the legislature reduced Crawford County to its present size and relocated the county seat to Steelville. County officials built a small, by modern standards, 29-foot-square courthouse there in 1839. These tight quarters served for eighteen years.

In 1857, citizens erected a second Steelville Courthouse of slightly larger dimensions. Fire destroyed this building in 1873. Eleven years later, the replacement courthouse also fell victim to fire.

In 1885, county officials occupied the present courthouse. It was enlarged by a major addition in 1974.

Top: Much of Crawford County's business is conducted over this counter. Family photos, greeting cards, obituaries, inspirational poems, thank-you notes, and political bric-a-brac entertain local residents who visit the courthouse to pay their taxes, question an assessment, or register to vote.

Bottom: The 1885 Crawford County Courthouse cost about $7,500. The two-story addition that extends to the east of the portico entry was added in 1974.

Dade County

Organized: January 29, 1841 |
County Seat: Greenfield | Architect:
Bonsack and Pearce

Top: The 1934 Dade County Courthouse was based on a 1922 proposal that had been postponed because the cost far exceeded the county's budget. A Work Projects Administration grant that surpassed the county's expectations by 300 percent allowed the more expensive version to go forward.

Bottom: Lisa Julian, deputy clerk, displays a painting of the courthouse that hangs in the county clerk's office. (From Dade County Collection. Artist: Gray Von Friedly, 1991)

In 1842, Dade County built its first courthouse, a one-and-a-half-story wood frame structure that was used until a more permanent courthouse was ready for occupancy around 1850. Civil War action destroyed that courthouse in 1863.

The county court constructed its third courthouse in 1868. After more than fifty years of service, a grand jury condemned this structure in 1921, but the court continued to use the dilapidated building for another four years.

In 1934, Dade County was an early participant in the Work Projects Administration program, and instead of the $36,000 grant it had expected, the county delightedly received $110,000 to build its new courthouse. County employees occupied their offices in the building in December 1935, and officials formally accepted the courthouse from the contractor in January 1936.

The 1956 Dallas County Courthouse in Buffalo is one of Missouri's post-war buildings. This view of the one-story, 121-foot-square building is from the third floor of the historic Laclede Hotel on the southwest corner of the square.

Dallas County

Organized: January 29, 1841 | County Seat: Buffalo | Architect: Eugene F. Johnson

In 1846, Dallas County citizens built their first courthouse. In 1863, at the height of the Civil War, Confederate troops burned that building.

Fire also destroyed the county's two subsequent temporary courthouses in 1864 and in 1867. The first permanent, post–Civil War courthouse was constructed in 1868. Sixty-nine years later, in 1937, that building was renovated. The cupola was removed in 1951. The building was destroyed by fire in 1955. The voters passed a bond issue later that same year for a replacement courthouse, and contracts were awarded in 1956.

The present courthouse was completed in 1958.

Daviess County

Organized: December 29, 1836 | County Seat: Gallatin | Architect: P. H. Weathers

In 1840, the county built itself a substantial foursquare courthouse. The foundation was three feet thick, the brick walls of the first floor were eighteen inches thick, and the second-story walls were thirteen inches thick. The building was stout.

It was colorful too. The walls and roof were Venetian red, doors were beech yellow, and the white window casings were accented with green blinds. However, as much a delight to the eye as it might have been, the building proved to be a maintenance catastrophe, and after years of complaints, it was razed in 1886.

Nearly twenty years would pass before the county successfully voted to build a replacement courthouse. Work on the current building began in 1906, and in 1907, officials conducted a cornerstone ceremony. County workers occupied the present courthouse for the first time in 1908.

Top: The 1906 Daviess County Courthouse is one of three courthouses that used a similar design by Architect Weather. The other two are in Cape Girardeau (1906) and Stoddard (1909) Counties.

Bottom left and right: The records in the office of Linda Adkins, clerk of the circuit court, include the execution order for Joseph Jump and John Smith. Jump and Smith played key but unfortunate roles at the county's last public hanging on May 28, 1886.

Top: The 1938 Dekalb County Courthouse was designed by the firm of Eckel and Aldrich. George R. Eckel was the son of an important Missouri architect, Edmond J. Eckel, who fifty-three years earlier had designed Dekalb County's 1885 courthouse.

Middle: The spire atop the tower of the 1885–1938 Dekalb County Courthouse was damaged by lightning in the early 1900s and removed.

Bottom: Mary Berry, Dekalb County Clerk, retrieves information needed to complete a grant application for a historic preservation project at the courthouse.

Dekalb County

Organized: February 25, 1845 | County Seat: Maysville | Architect: Eckel and Aldrich

Dekalb County officials built the county's first courthouse in 1851. Fire consumed that building in 1878 on Christmas Eve.

A replacement courthouse was constructed in 1885. The main entrance of this building was incorporated into the base of an off-center square tower. During the early 1900s, the tower's pyramidal spire was damaged by lightning and had to be removed.

Interestingly, the county jail at the rear of that building contained eight revolving cells in a lazy-Susan-type lockup. The cells had to be rotated to bring a cell into alignment with the single exit. The building was razed in 1938 to make way for its replacement.

Citizens authorized the present courthouse in 1938. Additional support was provided by a Work Projects Administration grant, and the courthouse was dedicated in 1939.

Dent County

Organized: February 10, 1851 | County Seat: Salem | Architect: Randolph Brothers

In 1851, Missouri legislators cut off the southern half of Crawford County and the northern half of Shannon County. The sum of land left from those subtractions became Dent County. A few more boundary modifications followed, and the county's present-day borders became firm in 1879.

Fire destroyed the county's first courthouse during the Civil War, and the second was destroyed immediately following the end of the conflict. The current courthouse was constructed in 1870.

An expansion in 1896 added a one-story addition at the rear of the building. In 1911, a second floor was added to that annex. More renovations during the 1930s created additional office space. In 1976, workers stripped yellow paint from the handmade, walnut stair railings, returning them to their natural color. The courthouse is listed on the National Register of Historic Places.

Top: In the 1920s, Dent County teachers taught in one-room schools. Standardized books, like the one shown here, were used to record test scores, grades, and progress notes for students ranging from first to seventh grades.

Middle: Dent County Clerk, Janet L. Inman, examines a 1920s school record book that tracked the progress of children attending several different grades in one of the county's one-room schools. At that time, counties were responsible for the operation of the schools that served Missouri's rural communities.

Bottom: The 1870 Dent County Courthouse design combines elements of several architectural styles, which was common for that period.

Douglas County

Organized: October 29, 1857 | County Seat: Ava | Architect: Dan R. Sanford

Douglas County officials picked Vera Cruz, a town located close to the county's geographic center, as their first county seat. In 1857, they erected a hewn-log courthouse. However, a few years later, after shells fell nearby during a Civil War scrimmage, the county seat was moved to Rome—a town near the southern border of the county. Sharp fighting then erupted around Rome as well, so the officials moved back to Vera Cruz, perhaps hoping that lightning would not strike the same spot twice.

The handsome, stone trim on the 1936 Douglas County Courthouse was made by mixing Carthage stone chips with cement and pouring the blend into blocks to harden. The blocks were polished to give them the look of quarried stone.

In 1872, competition for the county seat honor turned nasty. Residents of Arno, a rival community vying to be designated as county seat, stole the county records from the Vera Cruz Courthouse. The records were hidden away for two weeks.

The citizens of Militia Springs (renamed Ava in 1881) decided to intervene in the contest. In 1872, they built a courthouse and retrieved the records from Arno. The records were placed in a log vault, but in keeping with belligerent nature of the contest, vandals retaliated by burning the new Ava Courthouse and destroying many records.

The Ava officials rebuilt their courthouse in 1873. While tempers continued to simmer over the location of the county seat, the Ava Courthouse was put to the torch once again in 1886. However, the culprit was not a rival community but the county's assessor-treasurer seeking to destroy incriminating evidence of embezzlement. He was convicted and sentenced to five years. Contention over the location of the county seat continued into the early twentieth century, but the arguments did not involve other episodes of arson or kidnapping of county records.

In 1888, the county built a replacement courthouse in Ava that remained in use until 1936, when it was razed to make way for the current courthouse. The contractor began work on the new building in 1936, and the county officers and staff occupied the courthouse in January 1937.

Dunklin County

Organized: February 14, 1845 |
County Seat: Kennett | Architect:
Ernest T. Friton

Top: The 1937 Dunklin County Courthouse was constructed with a concrete framework that provides structural support for the two-story, brick building.

Bottom: A portrait of John Dalton, Missouri governor from 1961 to 1965, overlooks a map of Dunklin County that was inlaid in the mosaic floor of the courthouse. In 2005, the state designated the portion of U.S. Highway 412 that extends from the eastern city limits of Kennett to the western city limits of Hayti as the Governor John M. Dalton Memorial Highway.

In 1847, Dunklin County built a hewn-log courthouse that served until it was destroyed by a fire set during the Civil War. The replacement courthouse, built in 1870, also burned after only a couple of years as the seat of justice. Twenty years would pass before another replacement courthouse would be built.

In 1892, the county decided to build a new courthouse. By the 1930s, however, that courthouse was in desperate condition and needed replacement. The tower's dome had settled several inches, and various parts of the building were in danger of collapsing. In 1937, Dunklin County voters passed a bond issue for a new courthouse, and that appropriation was supplemented by a Work Projects Administration grant that covered two-thirds of the construction price. Construction began in 1937 and the building was completed in 1940.

An attractive map of Dunklin County, inlaid in the lobby's terrazzo floor, continues to draw the eye of visitors as they enter this courthouse.

Top: The second story of the Franklin County Courthouse was damaged in 1969 when brothers James and John Pardue set off a bomb as a diversionary tactic to draw attention away from their bank robbery that was in progress a few blocks from the courthouse. There were no fatalities, but several people in the courthouse were injured. The culprits were captured in 1971.

Middle: The 1847 Franklin County Courthouse was designed by Henry H. Wright, a popular Missouri architect who also designed similar courthouses for St. Francis (1848), Washington (1849), and Iron (1858) Counties. Iron County's courthouse is the only one still in use. (Courtesy: Franklin County Courthouse Collection. Photograph by F. T. Cooper)

Franklin County

Organized: December 11, 1818 | County Seat: Union | Architects: Norman Howard of Bonsack and Pearce

Franklin County's first county seat was at Newport between 1818 and 1826. The location of the town, near the Missouri River, proved to be an inconvenient spot for citizens living in the interior of the county. Legislators voted to move the county seat to Union, a town situated close to the geographic center of the county.

In 1827, a new courthouse was erected in Union, and it stood until 1849, when it made way for a replacement courthouse that had been started two years earlier. The replacement courthouse was razed in 1922.

Voters approved the present courthouse in 1921, and construction began in 1922. The building was dedicated in August 1923.

Bottom: This painting of past U.S. presidents hangs in the Franklin County commissioner's chambers. In 1969, it was shredded by an explosion, but the artist painstakingly restored the canvas and continued to add the faces of additional presidents until he retired in 1993. (Courtesy: Franklin County. Artist: Joseph D. McHugh)

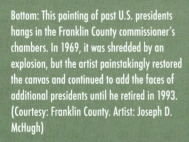

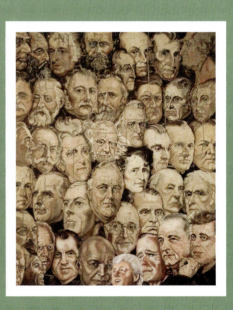

Gasconade County

Organized: November 25, 1820 | County Seat: Hermann | Architects: J. B. Legg and A. W. Elsner

Flooding and other problems caused Gasconade County officials to relocate the county seat to three different towns between 1821 and 1842 before selecting Hermann as their final choice. In 1842, Hermann's citizens constructed a foursquare building for their first courthouse, and perhaps the best decision they made concerning this building was to place it on a bluff with an extraordinarily commanding view of the Missouri River and the town of Hermann. In 1896, county officials ordered this building razed to make way for the courthouse that currently occupies the bluff site.

Charles D. Eitzen, a prominent Hermann merchant, left fifty thousand dollars in his will to pay for the replacement courthouse—making it the only courthouse in America built by a donation from a single individual. Workers began construction in 1897 and finished in 1898.

A fire in 1905 damaged the interior of the courthouse, but the building was quickly repaired. This building continues to serve as the Gasconade County seat of justice.

Top: In addition to the 1898 Gasconade County Courthouse, architect J. B. Legg used a similar design to construct the 1899–1997 Mississippi County and the 1901 St. Charles County courthouses.

Middle: Lisa Lietzow, Gasconade County Clerk, sits on an iron bench in the courthouse vestibule. The name of the courthouse's benefactor is emblazoned in gold letters on the bench. Eitzen and his wife are memorialized at several places throughout the building, including in a full length portrait in the courtroom.

Bottom left: The Gasconade County Circuit Court appears much as it did when it was restored following a fire in 1905. The underside of each seat has a wire rack for holding a gentleman's wide brimmed hat.

Bottom right: This painting shows a 1900 rendition of the courthouse and town of Hermann when stern-wheel riverboats still plied the Missouri River. A bridge now connects Gasconade County with Montgomery County at this point on the river. (Courtesy: Gasconade County. Artist: A. W. Miller)

Gentry County

Organized: February 14, 1845 | County Seat: Albany | Architect: Edmond J. Eckel

The increase in the number of new railroad lines into Missouri during the 1870s had a significant impact on the state's northern tier of counties. Only forty years earlier, Native Americans hunted buffalo on this land. The railroad lines opened new markets for cattle and grain farmers living in these relatively remote prairie communities, encouraging a new migration of settlers to the region and increasing the wealth of those already on the land.

A spur of the Chicago, Burlington, and Quincy Railroad reached Albany in 1879, and a second branch line was built at a point about two miles west of the town in 1881. These rail connections linked the county seat with major grain and cattle markets in the East, and Gentry County developed into a trading center for farming communities in northwestern Missouri.

In 1884, Gentry County built its current courthouse. This attractive building incorporates elements of the Second Empire style of architecture, making good use of a design style that was popular for public buildings during the later half of the nineteenth century.

The courthouse is listed on the National Register of Historic Places.

Top: The 1884 Gentry County Courthouse was built at a cost of $29,100. Edmond J. Eckel, a talented and highly respected architect, also designed the 1881 Nodaway, 1882 Atchison, and 1885 Dekalb Counties' courthouses, as well as hundreds of homes and business buildings in St. Joseph and northwest Missouri.

Bottom: The juxtaposition of the nineteenth century classic stamped ceiling tile with the twenty-first-century soft-drink machine in the Gentry County Courthouse entrance hall reminds visitors of the lifespan of historic courthouses.

Greene County

Organized: January 2, 1833 | County Seat: Springfield | Architects: A. N. Torbitt of Miller, Opel and Torbitt

James Campbell's parlor served as the site for early sessions of the Greene County court. He also donated fifty acres to the county for the court's use in raising funds to build public buildings. At the time, the practice of selling public or donated land and platted lots around the courthouse square was a common means of generating funds for public projects.

In 1836, the county officials began construction of the first courthouse on the new square, which was completed a few years later. After the passage of twenty-three years, the court ordered the worn-out building razed, but for some unknown reason the order was not carried out before the start of the Civil War. Prisoners of war were confined in the former courthouse, and later, someone decided to use it as a place to incarcerate a deranged fellow. This disturbed individual was not watched carefully during his confinement, however, and he set a fire that destroyed the building in October 1861.

Providentially, county officials had already ordered the construction of a new courthouse prior to these incidents. The replacement courthouse was a three-story building, a structural height that was rare for the time and that region of Missouri. It served the county until 1914.

In 1910, county officials authorized construction of the present courthouse. County officers moved into the building in 1912, but work continued until completion in 1915.

Top left: One of the drawings for the 1910 Greene County Courthouse included a tall central dome on the building, but due to financial restrictions, the optional dome and several other elements were eliminated from the finished building.

Top right: The 1838 Greene County Courthouse was a foursquare-style building topped by a cupola. (From: Springfield-Greene County Historic Museum exhibit. Artist: John Fulton)

Bottom: Greene County's courthouse rotunda stretches from the entry level to the third-floor dome skylight. Original plans called for a central tower above the rotunda, but that structure was not built.

Grundy County

Organized: January 29, 1841 | County Seat: Trenton | Architect: George A. Berlinghoff

In 1842, Grundy County built its first courthouse, a foursquare design with a tall cupola. At some point after the building was completed, Grundy County officials either ordered the cupola removed—perhaps due to leakage that was a common maintenance problem for cupolas and towers constructed during this time—or it was never installed in the first place. After sixty years of continuous service, the commissioners sold this building in 1902 and had it removed from the square.

In 1903, the county erected the current courthouse. The sixty thousand dollar bond issue was sufficient to pay for both a new courthouse and a separate jail. County commissioners supervised the work carefully, and expenses stayed within the budgeted amount. Both of the buildings were constructed of Bedford stone, also known as Indiana limestone. The stone was laid in alternating courses of rough and smooth surfaces.

The design of the jail building matches the courthouse. As was the custom of the day, the sheriff's family residence was located on the second story of the jail. In more recent time, however, as more women joined the jail population, the Sheriff's quarters were adapted to house female prisoners.

Top: The central tower on the Grundy County Courthouse stands 106 feet above street level. A sixty thousand dollar bond issue in 1903 was sufficient for both a new courthouse and a separate jail.

Bottom left: Specifications for the 1842–1902 Grundy County Courthouse called for the 13-foot-square base on the roof to be capped with a 21-foot-tall cupola, but the only illustration available shows only a square base without a cupola. (From: Grundy County Collection)

Bottom right: Carol Ausberger, deputy clerk, holds a slate roof tile painted with a likeness of the courthouse. Artist Esther Druckenmiller painted two dozen of the slate paintings to raise money for Trenton's sesquicentennial celebration in 2007. The original slate tiles were salvaged from a roof-repair project. (From: Missouri State Capitol. Lunette by Victor Higgins)

Harrison County

Organized: February 14, 1845 |
County Seat: Bethany | Architect:
Keene and Simpson

The town of Bethany used to be more centrally located, but in 1850, five years after Harrison County was organized, Missouri's new northern boundary received an additional strip of land six miles deep by twenty-four miles long. Consequently, Bethany was suddenly shifted south and away from its previously more central location in the county.

This move away from the central location and a spurt of population growth in the northern half of the county made the county seat vulnerable to challenges. During the next sixty years, two communities—Lorraine and Ridgeway—made a total of five separate attempts to win the honor of becoming the county seat, but all were unsuccessful.

In 1938, the county applied for a grant from the Work Projects Administration to build a new courthouse. The WPA projects were not noted for their decorative exuberance, but the circuit courtroom's pastel coloring and art deco ceiling fans are representative of the period. The marble interior walls also project a feeling of permanence and stability—highly desired attributes for government buildings. County officials occupied the building for the first time in 1940.

Top: The vertical, incised lines on the front exterior of the 1939 Harrison County Courthouse allude to the fluting on Doric columns, and carvings on the cornice run the circumference of the building. Several Work Projects Administration-funded courthouses incorporate these motifs in their generally streamlined design.

Middle: The ceiling fans and the pastel color of a Harrison County courtroom recall the Art Deco style of the 1920s.

Bottom: The corridor walls of the courthouse are covered floor to ceiling with polished stone cut to reveal its natural grain. The affability of the county's employees and elected officials creates an atmosphere of welcome and warmth that softens the efficient tone of the building.

Henry County

Organized: December 13, 1834 | County Seat: Clinton | Architects: Frederick C. Gunn and Louis S. Curtiss

In 1837, officials built the county's first courthouse. That building was condemned as unsafe in 1884, but it was not razed until three years later in 1887.

In 1891, Henry County voters approved a bond issue for construction of the present courthouse. The three-story building was built with Warrensburg sandstone, a popular stone that is quarried from a deposit that begins in Lafayette County and continues south through Johnson County (passing directly under the city of Warrensburg) and extends into the northern half of Henry County.

The courthouse was crowned by a monumental tower that unfortunately leaked from nearly the moment the workmen put away their tools. The tower's shell was made of a steel framework with a copper and stucco covering that was not watertight.

Repeated repairs failed to correct the problem, and in 1969, after the court informally surveyed the county's opinion, the tower was removed, albeit under protest from citizens who would have chosen to preserve it.

Hickory County

Organized: February 14, 1845 | County Seat: Hermitage | Architect: Unknown

In 1847, Hickory County built its first courthouse, but this building burned in 1852—sadly, only the first in a series of courthouse conflagrations that would plague the county. Eight years later in 1860, the county built its second courthouse only to watch that building go up in flames the same year.

County officials rallied to build a second 1860 courthouse. That building suffered storm damage in 1879 and was destroyed by fire in 1881—the last in a series of courthouse fires the county experienced. County officials decided to let fifteen years pass before beginning construction of another courthouse. Meanwhile, talk circulated about relocating the county seat, but the movement lacked sufficient support.

In 1896, officials built the current courthouse. Instead of a bond issue, citizen subscriptions paid the cost of the construction. The two-story, brick courthouse, with hip roof and open belfry, resembles the design of the 1860 building. In 1996, the Hickory County Courthouse installed indoor plumbing, allegedly becoming the last courthouse in Missouri to surrender its outdoor privy.

Top: With the exception of a one-story addition at the rear of the building, the exterior appearance of the 1896 Hickory County Courthouse remains unchanged. The 1896 building plan was based on its 1860 predecessor.

Middle: The commissioners' original minutes open with the April 1845 appointment of Jonas Brown as Hickory County's justice of the peace.

Bottom left: Kent Parson, Hickory County Clerk, is a lifelong resident and raconteur with stories about the life and times of people and events that have shaped the county.

Bottom right: Rolls of toilet paper dated with August 23, 1996, mark the installation of indoor plumbing at the Hickory County Courthouse.

Commemorative
Roll
Hickory County Outhouse
Wiped Out
Friday, August 23, 1996

Top: The 1965 Holt County Courthouse sits on one of the state's larger county squares. The square exceeds three hundred feet per side while most courthouse squares average between two hundred and three hundred feet per side.

Middle: Surveying the public land was an important step in settling Missouri. This 1849 Holt County township plat survey for Holt County was certified by Meriwether Lewis Clark, the son of William Clark and namesake of Clark's exploration partner, Meriwether Lewis. Clark assumed the surveyor general post in 1849, and his career also included work as an engineer and architect, Confederate officer in the Civil War, and commandant of cadets at the Kentucky Military Academy.

Holt County

Organized: January 29, 1841 | County Seat: Oregon | Architect: B. R. Hunter

In 1842, workers completed Holt County's first courthouse, a 20-by-26-foot, two-story building. Ten years later, the court moved into its second courthouse, a 46-foot-square, brick, two-story building that would be remodeled several times over the next 115 years.

In 1881, county officials ordered a major remodeling project that included adding a tower and mansard roof. Some people questioned why such an expensive project was not taken to the people for a vote of approval. The heated questions escalated into a vocal protest, which intensified into a lawsuit. The matter went to trial. In 1886, after appeals, the Missouri Supreme Court ruled in favor of the county officials, giving future elected officials better guidance as to which issues require voter approval.

In 1911, the building was again remodeled and several rooms were added. More additions followed during the 1930s. The building was painted gray and then white before its natural red brick was revealed around 1960. Fire destroyed the building in 1965.

The voters authorized a bond issue that same year to finance a replacement courthouse. In 1966, county officials occupied the current courthouse, and it continues to serve the people of Holt County.

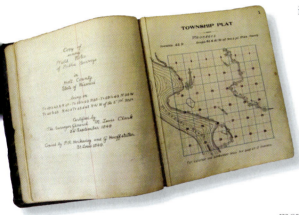

Bottom left: Sue Kneale, Holt County Clerk, responds to a constituent's question.

Bottom right: The 1850–65 Holt County Courthouse was remodeled in 1881 to a such degree that several disgruntled citizens filed a lawsuit claiming the county had constructed a new courthouse without seeking the approval of the people.

Howard County

Organized: January 23, 1816 | County Seat: Fayette | Architect: Schrage and Nickols

Howard County's first county seat was at Franklin, a town on the Missouri River. Officials soon moved the county seat to Fayette, and in 1823, they authorized construction of the first courthouse at that location. Most work on the building was completed in 1827, with finish plastering and window shutters added the following year. Fire destroyed the building in 1886.

In 1887, county residents approved construction of the present courthouse. In 1968, voters again approved a bond issue for renovation and remodeling of the aging building.

Calamity struck in 1975 when the old courthouse was gutted by fire. Only the walls remained. Workers managed to restore the exterior appearance of the building, but the original interior design was lost in the reconstruction.

Top: The 1887 Howard County Courthouse peeks through a grove of trees. Trees provide cooling shade and other benefits and contribute to the park-like setting favored by many county residents for their courthouse square.

Bottom left: The temple front 1857–86 Howard County Courthouse was destroyed by fire. White portico columns and pillars around the perimeter accented the red brick building. (From: Howard County Collection)

Bottom right: Howard County's first county seat was at the town of Franklin. In the lunette, a young girl covers her ears as a canon salutes the arrival of the first steam-powered boat to Franklin in 1819. (From: Missouri State Capitol. Lunette by Victor Higgins)

Howell County

Organized: March 2, 1857 | County Seat: West Plains | Architect: Earl Hawkins

Top: The Howell County Courthouse is an 82-foot-square, three-story, Carthage-stone building. The county had already accepted a plan for this courthouse in 1929 from architect Earl Hawkins to replace the existing building, but construction had to be delayed until 1935, when the voters passed a bond issue and a grant was approved by the WPA.

Middle: The 1882–1933 Howell County Courthouse was designed by Henry H. Hohenschild, who was only nineteen years old when he received the commission. (From: Howell County Collection, West Plains Bank 1980 promotion. Artist: James Burkhart)

Bottom: Dennis Von Allmen, Howell County Clerk, recalls the day in 1931 when Sheriff Roy Kelly died at the hands of Fred Barker, son of infamous bank robber Ma Barker from Oklahoma. Police raced to the gang's hideaway near Thayer in neighboring Oregon County after the shooting, but the outlaws had already fled the territory. Ma Barker and Fred were killed in a gun battle in Florida several years later.

On February 19, 1862, Union troops rode into West Plains on the heels of a cannon bombardment that damaged the courthouse. Before riding off again, the troops rounded up a few Rebel prisoners. In 1863, a band of Rebel guerilla fighters burned the entire town and completely devastated the county seat—not a single person remained in the town at war's end.

After the war, people drifted back to the county seat, and the county was formally reorganized by the legislature in 1866. A small courthouse was built in 1869 and served for thirteen years.

In 1882, voters authorized a fifteen thousand dollar appropriation for the third courthouse. The court selected Henry Hohenschild, a young talent just beginning his long and prolific career as the architect of a dozen Missouri courthouses.

Forty-six years later, a tragic event made it necessary to build yet another replacement courthouse for Howell County. In April 1928, a late-night explosion at a dancehall rocked the business district of West Plains. The force of the blast buckled the walls of the courthouse two blocks away. Thirty-six young men and women were killed by the blast—the cause of which is still a mystery. The forty-six-year-old courthouse walls were shoved out of alignment and threatened to topple at any time. The building was declared unsafe and razed in 1933.

In 1935, in need of a new courthouse and concerned that the Work Projects Administration program might be withdrawn, county officials rushed to submit an application. Fortunately, their plan was approved, and they were able to start work on the present courthouse. The new building was dedicated in June 1937. The building continues to serve the citizens of Howell County.

Iron County

Organized: February 17, 1857 | County Seat: Ironton | Architect: Henry H. Wright

In 1858, Iron County built its first and current courthouse. In 1964, a three-story addition was added to the rear of the building, extending its length by an additional forty-five feet. The building now measures about 50 by 110 feet, but otherwise the building is true to its original design.

Ironton was involved in the battle of Pilot Knob, and the courthouse suffered damage in that battle. In 1864, a strong force of Rebel troops attacked Union forces at the lightly defended Fort Davidson, an earthworks fort located a few miles northeast of Ironton. The Rebels were on a march to St. Louis in an effort to pull Union forces away from the eastern battlefields to defend their grip on the Mississippi River. Sterling Price, a former Missouri governor, led the southern troops.

On the second day of the battle, Confederate artillery hit the courthouse, which was being defended by Union troops at that point in the back-and-forth action. A cannonball crater can still be seen on the facade, above and to the right of the center window. Because of the stubborn resistance by the Federal troops, the Rebel army's drive north to St. Louis failed. Pilot Knob was the last major Civil War battle in Missouri.

The Iron County Courthouse is listed on the National Register of Historic Places.

Top: Scars from cannon and rifle fire inflicted on the Iron County Courthouse during the 1864 battle of Pilot Knob are still evident.

Bottom: On September 26, 1864, 1,450 Union troops blocked the advance of 12,000 Confederate soldiers marching toward St. Louis. Union troops made a brief stand at the courthouse before taking refuge at nearby Fort Davidson. The Rebel troops used the courthouse the next day as a hospital when they lost over 1,000 men in a bloody, but futile, attempt to overrun the fort. (Courtesy: "Thunder in Arcadia Valley: Price's Defeat September 27, 1864," by Bryce A. Suderow)

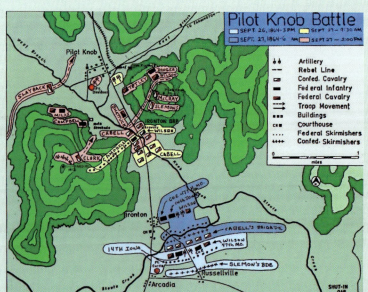

Jackson County

Organized: December 15, 1826 | County Seat: Independence | Architects: Wight and Wight; Keene and Simpson

Top: Lorenzo Ghiglieri's statue of Abraham Lincoln reading to his son Tad adds quiet dignity to the promenade that leads to the front entrance of the1933 Jackson County Courthouse in downtown Kansas City.

Bottom: WPA-era courthouses often evoke the art deco style of sleek, aerodynamic, rounded corners and parallel bands—sometimes called speed stripes—to communicate the theme of the streamlined government efficiency.

Right column

First: Archaeological discoveries early in the twentieth century, such as the tomb of King Tutankhamun, energized the design of public buildings during the 1920s and '30s.

Second: The lobby of the Jackson County Courthouse contains a rich mixture of color, mosaic, and polished stone.

Third: Future governor Lilburn Boggs supervised construction of Jackson County's 1828 courthouse, a temporary log structure. The log building was restored in 1916 as a tourist attraction but has since been destroyed. (Courtesy: Library of Congress)

Fourth: The Jackson County Courthouse in Independence now serves as a satellite of the downtown Kansas City Courthouse. Visitors to the building can tour the office used by Harry S. Truman when he began his political career as the presiding judge of Jackson County.

The county's first brick and stone building was completed in 1831, but due to faulty workmanship, the county court had to construct another building after only five years. The 1836 building received four major

renovations during the next ninety-five years. It was enlarged in 1852; a tower and east wing were added in 1872; and a courtroom was added in 1905. With its final renovation in 1933, it came to resemble Independence Hall. This courthouse is listed on the National Register of Historic Places.

In the 1870s, Kansas City outgrew Independence and needed its own courthouse. In 1872, county officials rehabilitated an unfinished hotel for court business. A tornado damaged this building in 1886.

In 1931, the county passed a bond issue that included four million dollars for a new courthouse. In 1933, construction began on the twenty-eight-story courthouse at Twelfth and Oak in downtown Kansas City. That building now serves as Jackson County's main courthouse.

Jasper County

Organized: January 29, 1841 | County Seat: Carthage | Architect: Maximilian A. Orlopp

Voters approved funding for the Jasper County Courthouse in May 1893. The cornerstone was laid August 21, 1894, and the building was dedicated October 9, 1895.

In 1842, Jasper County officials accepted a one-story, hewn-log building as their first courthouse. The county replaced that courthouse in 1854 with a foursquare-style, two-story, brick building that featured an observation platform on the roof instead of a cupola.

Civil War troops commandeered that courthouse and used it as a hospital for a while, but it was destroyed by fire in 1863. For the next thirty years, the county functioned without a courthouse and county business was conducted at temporary quarters around the town square.

In 1891, the county decided it was time to build a new courthouse, and the court approached the challenge with flair, agreeing to build two courthouses. The county seat courthouse would be a joint project with the city of Carthage. The second courthouse would be built at Joplin, about fifteen miles to the southwest, to facilitate circuit court sessions in that city. Voters approved the ambitious plan, but the citizens of Webb City protested that they had been slighted in the decision regarding where to locate the second courthouse. After the Missouri Supreme Court ruled on the case, the bond issue was re-submitted to the voters. The issue passed a second time, and with the Webb City challenge settled, construction of the two courthouses was completed in 1893.

The Joplin Courthouse, however, was destroyed by fire on June 14, 1911, and was not rebuilt.

Construction of the Jasper County Courthouse in Carthage involved ongoing disagreements between architect M. A. Orlopp and construction supervisor Nelson L. Damon. The acrimony between the two men became public and was reported in the local newspapers. Damon, for example, argued that excavations for the building's foundation should continue until they reached bedrock, while Orlopp insisted that digging to such depth was unnecessary. The rancorous relationship between the designer and the builder may have slowed construction, but the finished building is still considered one of the finest of its type in Missouri. It is listed on the National Register of Historic Places.

Top: The wheeled cart used for transporting heavy record books around the courthouse was the nineteenth century's answer to high-speed data transfer. The painting by Lowell Davis depicts the 1854–63 Jasper County Courthouse.

Bottom: When the court proposed building a new courthouse at Carthage in 1891, it decided to build a second courthouse in Joplin at the same time. (From: Jasper County Collection)

Jefferson County

Organized: December 8, 1818 | County Seat: Hillsboro | Architect: Charles H. Pond (1863); Bruce Barnes and Associates (1954 renovation)

Jefferson County is one of Missouri's most senior counties. Herculaneum, a town located on the Mississippi River, was chosen as the first county seat. No courthouse was built there, however, and the court met at any facility that was available—a common procedure at the time. Lead from the mines at Potosi was shipped overland to Herculaneum for transportation downriver. The town supplied most of the lead used by the United States to make musket shot and cannon balls during the War of 1812.

Herculaneum's location as county seat proved to be unpopular, however, and in 1838, the newly established town of Hillsboro was selected as the new county seat. The following year, the court ordered the construction of a brick courthouse and jail. This building served the community for a quarter century until it was replaced by the 1863 courthouse.

A freestanding, fireproof annex was added at the east side of the courthouse in 1892, and the buildings were connected by a second-story walkway. In 1952, the courthouse was significantly altered in size and appearance by the addition of wings to each side of the core building. That building remains in service but is used exclusively for court activities; county administrative offices have been relocated to separate quarters.

Top: The scale of Justice, carved in the stonework above the entry, marks the remaining portion of the 1863 courthouse. During the last 140-plus years, the building has been expanded and remodeled several times.

Bottom: Herculaneum was Jefferson County's first county seat. The river community was founded in 1808 by Moses Austin to process ore from his mines at Mine a Breton. (From: Missouri State Capitol. Lunette by O. E. Berninghous, 1924)

Top: A statue of Minerva stands atop the 1896 Johnson County Courthouse. The courthouse and statue were restored in 1994–96.

Middle: The 1838–78 Johnson County Courthouse was the site of Senator George Graham Vest's famous "Tribute to a Dog," which he used as his closing argument in the *Burden v. Hornsby* trial.

Bottom: Johnson County Deputy Clerks Sarah Welsh (left) and Christy Lile enjoy one of the perks of their job as they examine copies of historic specification sheets used for construction of the 1896 courthouse. The folder is then returned to its storage place in the commissioner's chamber.

Johnson County

Organized: December 13, 1834 | County Seat: Warrensburg | Architect: George E. McDonald

Johnson County's first courthouse (1838–78) survives today due to the restoration and preservation efforts of the Johnson County Historical Society. The foursquare style was one of the most popular designs used for courthouses during the nineteenth century, but the Johnson County building is the only remaining example of its type in Missouri.

County commissioners used the large first-floor courtroom for meetings when the circuit court was not in session. Four fireplaces at the four corners of the building heated the room. Offices on the second floor provided working space and record storage room for the county clerk, assessor, collector, and other county officials. The Johnson County Historical Society has restored the building to its original specifications and furnished it with appropriate period pieces. The building has been added to the National Register of Historic Places and is now used as a museum.

In 1896, Johnson County constructed the current courthouse. Made with locally quarried sandstone, the building is the first of four Missouri courthouses designed by architect George E. McDonald of Omaha, Nebraska. Completed in 1898, the Romanesque-designed courthouse continues to serve the people of Johnson County and is also listed on the National Register of Historic Places.

Knox County

Organized: February 14, 1845 | County
Seat: Edina | Architect: William B. Ittner

In 1848, Knox County officials built the county's first courthouse, a simple, two-story, 40-by-30-foot building. Fire destroyed that building on Christmas Eve 1885. Arson was strongly suspected, but no arrests were ever made. The county functioned without a courthouse

for the next forty-nine years. In 1934, a committee charged with exploring the possibility of securing a Work Projects Administration grant commissioned preliminary sketches from a St. Louis architect. It submitted these plans to the WPA and then waited until it received approval from Washington before it announced the proposition of building a new courthouse to the public.

The voters passed the bond issue as required, and with complete funding assured, Knox County officials formally approved the architect's design and quickly ordered work to begin on the building. Thus, a clandestine meeting with an architect early in 1934—a maneuver that would have attracted criticism under other circumstances—led to a dedication ceremony of the new courthouse only fourteen months later, in September 1935.

Top: Total cost for construction of the 1934 Knox County Courthouse was about eighty thousand dollars, an amount equal to the WPA grant the county secured before taking the issue to the voters.

Middle: In 1935, Knox County elected officials gathered on the steps of their new courthouse. The building had been formally dedicated nine days earlier. (From: Knox County Collection. Photograph by H. A. Insinger)

Bottom left: The Knox County Historical Museum is located in one of the lower level rooms in the courthouse. Small-town marching bands, tunefully immortalized by Meredith Willson's 1957 Broadway musical, *The Music Man*, were popular in small-town America at the turn of the twentieth century, and this uniform dates from that era.

Bottom right: Civil War veterans' organizations celebrated their service by marching in annual Memorial Day parades. This flag was proudly carried by elderly soldiers, one after another, until all had passed from the scene. This ensign is part of the Knox County Historical Society's courthouse museum collection.

Top: The 1924 Laclede County Courthouse was rebuilt in 1998 to enable a correct matchup with the expansion project being built adjacent to the courthouse. Workers refused to enter the old courthouse after portions of the building's support beams crumbled, exposing rebar and deteriorated concrete.

Bottom: Laclede County Clerk Glenda Mott is responsible for the storage of records relating to road and bridge work in the county. These 1935 blueprints were used during an improvement project on a portion of old Route 66 that runs near Lebanon.

Laclede County

Organized: February 24, 1849 | County Seat: Lebanon | Architect: Earl Hawkins

In 1851, Laclede County built its first courthouse in Lebanon. The courthouse, a one-and-a-half-story frame building, served the community for about twenty years. When the time approached for that building to be replaced, a question about the location of the county seat generated a protracted debate. The argument began in 1868, when a railroad line was built near Lebanon but bypassed the old town center by about a mile. The town's merchants began moving their establishments to be near the railroad depot, and soon Lebanon's entire business district had relocated, leaving the courthouse surrounded by empty buildings and a deserted town square.

In 1894, yielding to the reality of the situation, county officials abandoned their old county seat site and ordered the next courthouse to be built at the town's new location.

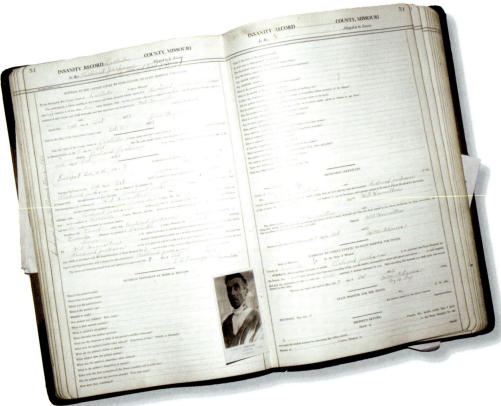

That courthouse burned in 1920. Citizens defeated the court's first bond issue for a replacement building because they thought it too expensive. In 1924, voters approved a more modest plan, and the current courthouse was completed the following year.

By 1994, this courthouse showed its age. County officials submitted a plan to the voters, and they authorized the renovation of the old courthouse along with a simultaneous expansion project that would add new office and judicial space. The project began in 1995.

Workers halted the courthouse renovation phase of the project, however, when they discovered that the building was unsafe. After studying the situation, the solution chosen was to demolish the old courthouse and replace it with an identical version of itself. This seemingly contradictory move was necessary so that the expansion part of the overall project, which was already well underway, would connect properly with the courthouse as planned. The new complex was dedicated in 2000.

Top left: Odds are good that the cannonball in the column is a Yankee shot, because the Confederate headquarters were near the courthouse during the Battle of Lexington and General Sterling Price would have made a tempting target for the Union artillery.

Top right: The 1847 Lafayette County Courthouse, a temple-front building, was built at a cost of twelve thousand dollars.

Bottom: Union forces surrendered to the Confederate troops in Lexington on September 20, 1861, but the victory did not lead to Missouri seceding from the Union as the Rebels had hoped. (From: Lafayette County Historical Society Collection. Artist: Joe Oliard, 1979)

Lafayette County

Organized: November 16, 1820 | County Seat: Lexington | Architect: William Daugherty

In 1825, county officials constructed their first courthouse in Lexington, and that building remained in use until 1832. The replacement courthouse, a three-story building, was completed in 1835. After ending its tenure as a courthouse in 1849, that building was subsequently used as a school and commandeered into service as a troop hospital during the Civil War.

Voters authorized the present courthouse in 1847, and it was completed in 1849. In 1854, the court added a small annex for the clerk's office. In 1861, during the Battle of Lexington, a cannon ball became embedded in one of the columns—where it remains to this day. In 1854, the court added a wing for offices on the east side of the building. During the 1880s, workers added a second floor to the wing, creating a two-story annex. In 1939, the county secured a Work Projects Administration grant to connect the annex to the main courthouse and add new vaults and offices. Lafayette County's courthouse is the oldest courthouse remaining in use in Missouri.

The building is listed on the National Register of Historic Places.

Lawrence County

Organized: February 14, 1845 | County Seat: Mount Vernon | Architect: George McDonald

In 1846, Lawrence County officials built their first courthouse, a two-story frame building with an 18-by-30-foot base. Only seven years later, the court erected a replacement courthouse. That building was originally planned as a two-story structure, but after the local Masonic Lodge signed a lease with the county, the court decided to add a third floor. Fire destroyed the building near the end of the nineteenth century.

In 1900, the voters authorized construction of the current courthouse, and construction on the building was completed that same year. Before the days of central heating, Lawrence County employees warmed themselves on cold winter days by holding their hands in front of blazing fireplaces that were located in the four corners of each floor.

This Lawrence courthouse never suffered a major fire, but such fireplaces in other courthouses were the culprits behind many of the devastating fires that destroyed many Missouri courthouses throughout the nineteenth and early twentieth centuries.

REMEMBER LAWRENCE!!!

Don't give up the Ship.

WANTED
FOR THE
U. S. NAVY,
SEAMEN,
ORDINARY SEAMEN,
AND GREEN HANDS,
For seagoing Ship Pennsylvania and all others, such as 74's, frigates and Sloops of war.

Good Wages
FOR
GOOD MEN.
APPLY TO
JOHN C. RIGHTER,
Shipping Master of the U. S. Navy, No. 162 South Front Street.

Top: Passage of the bond issue to build the 1900 Lawrence County Courthouse was so popular that a band played "Hot Time in the Old Town Tonight" when it heard the news. One veteran courthouse employee recalls the 1940s, when it was an annual Thanksgiving tradition for Lawrence County office holders to toss live turkeys from a second-story window to the crowd below on the lawn.

Middle: Captain Lawrence's famous cry, "Don't Give Up the Ship," became the Navy's motto and was featured on recruitment posters. (From: Lawrence County Collection)

Bottom left: Gary Emerson, Lawrence County Clerk (left), and Fred Mieswinkel, Deputy Clerk in the recorder's office, chat in front of one of the courthouse's fireplaces.

Bottom right: The 1853–95 Lawrence County Courthouse served as a backdrop for a man with a young girl displaying his horse and carriage near the courthouse square in Mount Vernon. This photograph is one of several recovered from a time capsule placed with the 1900 courthouse's cornerstone. (From: Lawrence County Collection)

Lewis County

Organized: January 2, 1833 | County Seat: Monticello | Architect: J. T. McAllister

In 1834, Lewis County officials built their first courthouse, a rustic one-room, hewn-log building that was meant to be only a temporary home for the court. The court had to borrow one hundred dollars to pay the builder for his work when it was completed. Five years later, the court replaced its log courthouse with a two-story, brick building. This structure served the county for about thirty-six years, and it was replaced by the current courthouse it in 1875.

The 1875 courthouse has received minor additions, but the original design of the building has not been altered significantly during the past 130 years. A small, one-story office annex now stands on the square a short distance from the east side of the courthouse.

Top: Decorative brickwork and paired brackets along the cornice enrich the facade of the 1875 Lewis County Courthouse.

Bottom left: The first will filed in Lewis County, submitted to the probate court on February 10, 1834, is still on file and available for public review at the courthouse 172 years later.

Bottom right: Janet Chapman's assignment is to digitally scan the Lewis County probate records to make them accessible by computer and protect the original copies. Some of these files date to 1833.

Lincoln County

Organized: December 14, 1818 | County Seat: Troy | Architect: Gustave Bachmann

Monroe, a town near Lincoln County's southeastern border, was the county's first choice as the county seat. However, people considered it inconveniently located. In 1823, county officials selected Alexandria as a replacement site. The court built a small frame courthouse there, but the site did not meet with favor, and citizens petitioned the court to move the county seat to Troy in 1829.

In 1830, the county built its first courthouse in Troy, a foursquare building that remained in use until 1869, when it was razed to make way for a replacement courthouse.

The current courthouse was built in 1870.

WOOD'S FORT-1812-NOW TROY-IN LINCOLN COUNTY

Top: The 1869 Lincoln County Courthouse has been expanded several times with annexes and additions but continues to retain its Georgian style of architecture that was popular for courthouses in Missouri's "Little Dixie" region during the middle part of the nineteenth century.

Bottom: During the War of 1812, Native American tribes were British allies and tried to expel settlers from their hunting grounds. Woods Fort in Lincoln County was one of the several Missouri forts built for protection against attacks. Woods Fort grew to become the frontier community of Troy, the county seat after 1829. (From: Missouri State Capitol. Lunette by William Knox)

Top: Deputy Sheriff Herb Boedeker provides security and welcomes visitors to the courthouse from his station in the lobby. The staircases and zinc ceiling tiles are two of the architectural highlights of the building.

Bottom: Lincoln County's first organizational meeting was held at Zadock Woods's farmhouse on April 5, 1819. The business recorded in these minutes included setting election dates and making other preparations necessary to start a county government that has gone on to function effectively for nearly two hundred years.

The building has been modified several times over the years. Two additions have expanded the footprint of the building, one in the 1930s and another in 1974. In 1984, several vaults were installed and offices were remodeled. In 1991, the building received an elevator and other accessibility improvements, new and remodeled office spaces, and plant improvements, including heating and air-conditioning equipment and roof repairs. More improvements were made in 1996. The historic 1870s-era courthouse continues to serve the people of Lincoln County.

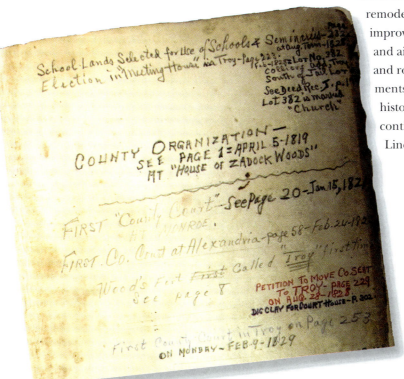

Linn County

Organized: January 6, 1837 | County Seat: Linneus | Architects:
Rae Sanneman and R. W. Van Trump

In 1841, county officials built their first courthouse, a two-story, hand-hewn log building. A second courthouse replaced this building in 1848. The replacement courthouse was repaired

in 1857 and remodeled in 1867 but remained in such poor condition that it was rated unsafe for occupancy in 1879. County officers moved out of the building, but repairs and remodeling efforts kept at least part of the building open for business into the twentieth century.

Citizens petitioned the court for a new courthouse, and a bond issue was added to a special August 1, 1911, ballot. The special election was a statewide issue to approve appropriations for a new state capitol. The Missouri Capitol had been destroyed by fire earlier that same year. Supporters of Linn's courthouse issue believed the county's bond issue would stand a better chance of passage if it took advantage of the enthusiasm generated for building a new capitol. The strategy proved successful, and the Linn County levy passed. Citizens celebrated with enthusiasm when the results were announced.

In 1913, county commissioners signed the construction contract for the new building, and it was dedicated in 1914. The ninety-three-year-old building remains in service for the people of Linn County.

Top: An elevator shaft installed next to the main entrance on the west side of the 1915 Linn County Courthouse increased handicapped accessibility to the upper floors.

Bottom left: Peggy Ward, Linn County Clerk, stores historic county records in a climate-controlled storage building. Humidity and temperature control are important factors when preserving records.

Bottom right: Loretta Brookshier, Recorder of Deeds, compares an 1857 warranty land deed record book with a 2006 computerized facsimile. Linn County's paper deeds are scanned and digitally stored, and some counties have switched entirely to electronic filing, eliminating the need for paper originals altogether.

Livingston County

Organized: January 6, 1837 | County Seat: Chillicothe | Architects: Warren Roberts and George Saase

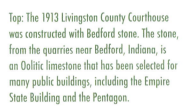

Top: The 1913 Livingston County Courthouse was constructed with Bedford stone. The stone, from the quarries near Bedford, Indiana, is an Oolitic limestone that has been selected for many public buildings, including the Empire State Building and the Pentagon.

Bottom: Virgil Werteen, a member of the Livingston County maintenance staff, positions a photograph of the county's first courthouse that hangs in the circuit courtroom. The hewn-log building was used as a schoolhouse after being used for only a few years as the courthouse.

In 1837, Livingston County officials held their first sessions in a windowless log building. Suffering the gloom for four years, the court moved in 1841 to a more commodious, four-square courthouse located on the square. That building was deemed unsafe and razed in 1864.

After the old courthouse was removed, the square stood empty for nearly fifty years. County business was conducted at various locations around town, and the community used the courthouse square as a park. During this time, voters rejected several bond issues to build a replacement courthouse.

In 1912, voters finally approved a new courthouse. The design selected for the building draws on classic style and was a very popular style in Missouri between the years 1910 to 1930. The county accepted the completed building from the builder in 1913, and it remains an active courthouse.

McDonald County

Organized: March 3, 1849 | County Seat: Pineville | Architect: Hood-Rich, Architects and Consulting Engineers

Shortly after the county was organized, the competition between towns over who would be named as the county seat turned deadly. Ruffians from the rival communities of Rutledge and Pineville fought over the question; and in 1850, during a melee in Rutledge, three men were killed when the argument became violent. Tempers were still simmering six years later, when vandals destroyed a log courthouse in Rutledge—another incident in a list of skirmishes that embroiled the two towns. Divided by the issue of slavery and free soil, the two communities established separate courthouses, complete with their own set of county officials. Neither side would yield.

In 1857, state authorities intervened to stop the violence and confusion caused by having two county seats. Pineville was named as the official county seat, and a new courthouse was built in that town in 1858. The county built a replacement courthouse in 1861, but a couple of years later, that building was burned by Bushwhackers during the Civil War.

Without a courthouse, the county rented one for a few years. In 1870, the court began construction of a two-story, brick building that was completed in 1871. In 1938, the courthouse

played a supporting role in a Twentieth Century Fox film about Jesse James that was filmed on location in Pineville. The building still stands on the old square in downtown Pineville, but it is no longer used as the courthouse.

In 1977, the court purchased a lot several blocks north of the square as a site for the present courthouse. The one-story, 5,500-square-foot facility was constructed and accepted by the county in 1978.

Top: The 1977 McDonald County Courthouse received funding from the Local Public Works Capital Development and Investment Act of 1977, as amended by the Public Works Employment Act of 1977, under the U.S. Department of Commerce.

Bottom: The 1870–1978 McDonald County Courthouse remains on the old county square in Pineville. A one-story addition was added in 1905, and the brick building was covered in stucco and painted white in 1943.

Macon County

Organized: January 6, 1837 |
County Seat: Macon | Architect:
Levi Aldrich

The town of Bloomington served as Macon County's first county seat, and the courthouse built there in 1838 was a two-story, hewn-log affair that was intended only as a temporary facility. Three years later, the county erected its first permanent courthouse, a foursquare-style building.

Top: The land for the 1865 Macon County Courthouse was donated to the county by James Terrell. The second-story courtroom is noted for its excellent acoustics.

Bottom: This round attorney's table is original court furniture from the 1865 courthouse. Pat Clarke, county clerk (left) and Cindy Kennel Ayers, juvenile officer for Macon and Shelby Counties, hold a 1900 photograph of the courtroom that shows the same 1860s table.

During the Civil War, Union General Lewis Merrill was in control of northern Missouri, and he thought Bloomington was a town filled with Southern sympathizers. His troops were being harried by bushwhackers who were difficult to catch because they disappeared into the local population after conducting raids against his troops. General Merrill ordered his men to burn the town in retaliation.

Before the order could be carried out, however, one of Merrill's officers suggested a less harsh but, in the long run, even crueler penalty. He recommended that Merrill strip the town of its county seat designation and move the Macon County government in another town. In 1863, state legislators complied and moved the county seat to Macon City. Bloomington, a town that had served as the county seat for nearly thirty years in Macon County, lost its reason for existence and eventually disappeared from the map.

In 1865, officials constructed the first and only courthouse in Macon. The annex building was added in 1895. Macon officials made a serious attempt to build a replacement courthouse in 1938, but even with the WPA grant already secured, they could not begin construction within the required nine week time limit, and they had to cancel the project.

The 140-year-old building is listed on the National Register of Historic Places.

Madison County

Organized: December 14, 1818 | County Seat: Fredericktown | Architect: Theodore C. Link

In 1822, Madison County officials constructed the court's first courthouse, a foursquare-style, 50-foot-square, two-story building that included a hip roof and cupola. That sturdy building, constructed with handmade bricks, continued in use until 1899, when the county paid Mr. J. F. Boggs twenty-five dollars to demolish it in order to make way for its replacement.

In 1899, voters approved construction of the present courthouse. The red-brick structure's central tower is located over the south entrance of the building, and it continues to serve as the seat of justice for Madison County.

Top: The 1899 Madison County Courthouse was built by Mr. Lewis Miller, a contractor from nearby Iron County. His low bid was about $18,100, but final costs amounted to approximately $22,000.

Middle: The courtroom, about fifty-two foot square, is located on the second floor. The balcony is no longer used for seating.

Bottom left: Madison County Clerk Joan Whitener compares a computer-generated county map with a hand-drawn version that hangs in the lobby of the Fredericktown Courthouse.

Bottom right: In 1717, shortly before being recalled to France, Lamothe Cadillac, then governor of Louisiana, explored for silver but discovered lead instead at Mine La Motte—a site four miles south of Fredericktown, the present county seat. (From: Missouri State Capitol. Lunette by O. E. Berninghous, 1924)

Maries County

Organized: March 2, 1855 | County Seat: Vienna | Architect: Macon C. Abbitt

In 1856, Maries County built its first courthouse, a tidy, brick, two-story building that survived the Civil War but, nevertheless, burned in 1868 at the hands of an arsonist. In 1870, the court completed construction of a replacement courthouse. That building continued in use until it was time to make way for a twentieth-century replacement.

In 1939, Maries County officials put the question of whether or not to build a new courthouse to county residents. The Work Projects Administration had agreed to fund 55 percent of the construction cost of a new building, but the county was required to pass a levy to fund the difference. The local newspaper editorialized in favor of passage of the bond issue, cautioning readers that the WPA grants might not be available much longer.

Voters heeded the prophetic advice and approved the bond issue in January 1940. The building was completed in 1942. The sixty-six-year-old courthouse continues to serve the citizens of Maries County.

Marion County

Organized: December 23, 1826 | County Seat: Palmyra | Architect: William N. Bowman

Marion County officials began making plans for a courthouse in 1828, but unsettled land title questions prompted them to wait. Two years later, the title questions were resolved and the court was ready to begin construction of the county's first courthouse. The county accepted the building in 1832, but finish work slowed the completion date until 1835.

In 1853, the courthouse was removed to make way for its replacement. The second courthouse, begun in 1853, was ready for occupancy in 1855. The tower was capped with a four-foot-diameter, silver-painted, metal ball.

Top: Few courthouses display all of the characteristics made popular by architect H. H. Richardson, but the 1900 Marion County Courthouse includes several of the details that found wide public favor, such as a central tower and large, round, arched, recessed entries. The courthouse is, however, lighter in color and uses ashlar masonry (smooth, cut stone) rather than rusticated stonework and, so, does not appear as heavy as most Richardsonian Romanesque buildings.

Bottom: The design for the 1853–1900 Marion County Courthouse called for a temple front to the building, but the characteristic porch and columns were never added.

During the Civil War, this shining ball was an irresistible target for sharpshooters who wished to prove their marksmanship.

Marion County has two courthouses. In 1844, the court established a Court of Common Pleas in Hannibal to deal with maritime law cases associated with traffic on the nearby Mississippi River. Over the next several years, as Hannibal grew in population, the court's duties were expanded to include probate matters and Municipal Court cases.

By 1899, it was clear that the Palmyra Courthouse needed repair, and that a better courthouse arrangement in Hannibal would improve that court's efficiency as well. In 1900, the question went before the voters, and they agreed to build new courthouses in Palmyra and Hannibal.

Progress on the Palmyra Courthouse was briefly stymied while Bowman, the architect, wrangled with his former employer over the ownership rights to his plans for the new building.

Top: Robert J. Ravenscraft, County clerk, poses with the large ball that was atop the 1853–1900 courthouse. The holes in the ball were made by Rebel sharpshooters who used the ball for target practice. Ravenscraft traveled to Albania in 1997 and Russia in 1999 as a part of an international team to monitor elections in those former Soviet Union countries.

Middle: County elections epitomize Missouri grassroots politics. Jean Buckman, Marion County treasurer, holds a collection of presidential campaign buttons from bygone elections.

Bottom: Marion County's second courthouse, located in Hannibal, was built in 1900 as part of the same bond election that paid for the courthouse in Palmyra. The 1906 Boone County Courthouse resembles the portico-fronted Hannibal Courthouse.

Marion County officials sided with the architect and paid him for his work.

The Hannibal Courthouse project, designed by architect James O. Hogg, went more smoothly. The county accepted both buildings in the summer of 1901, and they continue in use today.

Mercer County

Organized: February 14, 1845 | County Seat: Princeton | Architects: R. W. Van Trump and Rae Sanneman

In 1847, the county raised money for public buildings by selling lots from the forty acres of land it had purchased from the federal government. Some of that money was used to build the county's first courthouse, a two-story, hewn-log building. In 1858, it built a replacement courthouse, made from brick, in the center of the town square. After forty years of operation, that building was destroyed by fire.

The county functioned without a courthouse while a levy to build a new courthouse was rejected by voters six different times. Finally, in 1911, citizens authorized an appropriation to build the county's present courthouse. The cornerstone ceremony was held on June 8, 1912, and the building was completed in April 1913. The county continues to use this building as its seat of justice.

Top: Voters passed a seventy-five thousand dollar bond issue to construct the 1912 Mercer County Courthouse. The county had been without a courthouse since 1898, and the courthouse square had been turned over to the city for a park. Princeton residents donated another four thousand dollars to purchase a nearby lot for the new courthouse.

Middle: The Mercer County Commission in session—Deputy Clerk Darlene McReynolds (left), Associate Commissioner Kenneth Wilson, Associate Commissioner Shane Grooms, Presiding Commissioner Clifford Shipley, and County Clerk Carolyn Kost.

Bottom: Jury rooms are unused and empty, waiting until the next trial. Once a trial is competed and deliberations begin, jury members are confined to the jury room until they reach a verdict or are excused by the judge.

Miller County

Organized: February 6, 1837 | County Seat: Tuscumbia | Architect: Archetype Design Group Inc.

Top: The 2003 Miller County Courthouse is located on new ground, about a half-mile northwest of the old square. EBCO Construction Group, Olathe, Kansas built the building.

Bottom: The north and south wings and limestone veneer were added to the 1858 Miller County Courthouse in 1909.

In 1840, Miller County built its first courthouse, a hand-hewn log structure with a stone foundation and rough plank floor. The builder continued his finish work into 1841, but despite repairs that were made to the building in 1843 and again in 1847, it was never considered satisfactory. The county clerk tried twice to find other accommodations. In 1858, the building was auctioned to the highest bidder.

Citizens petitioned for a replacement courthouse in 1856, and after the court appropriated an initial four thousand dollars toward the six thousand dollar construction cost, work began on a new building in 1857. The bricks used for the project were manufactured locally, but the masonry was of such poor quality that immediately upon accepting the building in 1859, the court ordered the building to be painted with two coats of red paint.

There were several attempts to replace this building early in the twentieth century, but bond issues repeatedly failed at the ballot box. Finally, in 1909, the court decided to remodel the existing facility rather than build a new building. The commissioners doubled the size of the building by adding 28-by-50-foot wings to the north and south sides of the core building. In 1910, they covered the exterior with native limestone, and work on the building was completed in 1913. Abandoned early in the twenty-first century, the courthouse was sold and is now in private ownership.

In May 2003, the county dedicated its current courthouse and law enforcement center. The land for the previous courthouse was sold along with the building, necessitating purchase of land a short distance away for construction of the new courthouse.

Mississippi County

Organized: February 14, 1845 | County Seat: Charleston | Architects: Mary A. Bell of William A. Green and Associates Inc.

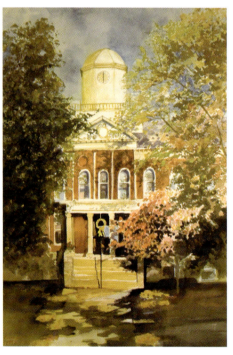

The county constructed a building to house the county clerk's office in 1846, but Mississippi County did not build its first courthouse until 1852. This two-story, frame building served for thirty-nine years but was destroyed by fire in 1891. The county utilized temporary quarters in buildings around the square until 1900.

In 1899, the Mississippi County voters approved construction of a new courthouse. The Mississippi County Courthouse was completed in 1901. Tragically, this historic and stately building was destroyed by an arsonist's fire on February 10, 1997.

The present courthouse was built on the same site and dedicated in 1999. William A. Green and Associates Inc. was the engineer and architect, along with architect Mary A. Bell. C. A. Walker Construction Company of Dexter, Missouri, was the contractor.

Top: The 1999 Mississippi County Courthouse design captures memories of the county's storied past by including details reminiscent of the classic nineteenth-century courthouses, such as a porticoed entrance, clock, and cupola. The building's foundation stands on a compacted, earthquake-resistant fill designed to help the structure remain upright if the New Madrid Fault becomes active again.

Bottom: This watercolor shows details of the 1899 courthouse's main entrance. The 1899–1997 Mississippi County Courthouse was designed by architect Jerome Legg, and it was similar in appearance to two other courthouses that he designed in St. Charles (1901) and Gasconade (1898) Counties. (Courtesy: Mississippi County Collection. Artist: D. Gross, 1999)

Moniteau County

Organized: February 14, 1845 |
County Seat: California | Architect:
Unknown (1867); O. E. Sprouce
(1905 remodel)

Top and middle: In 1905, the cupola was heightened, and a dome was added to the portico of the1867 Moniteau County Courthouse. These modifications were influenced by similar design changes that had been made to the portico and dome on the old State Capitol building in Jefferson City a few years earlier.

Bottom left: Don Osborn, seventy-seven, is a local resident, and a retired radio personality whose program *Garden Of Oz* was heard on more than 260 radio stations during the 1990s. The Native American artifacts were collected locally. "Moniteau" is the French spelling of the Native American word that means "spirit" or "God."

Bottom right: Harold Haldiman (foreground), County treasurer, confers with Tony Barry (left) and Kim F. Roll, associate commissioners, and Kenneth Kunze, presiding commissioner.

In 1846, the county cleared the recently surveyed one-acre public square in preparation for construction of the first courthouse, a brick, two-story building with a stone foundation. That courthouse served the county until 1867, when the square was cleared once again in preparation for a new courthouse.

The contract for building the current courthouse was awarded in April 1867, and construction was completed the following February. The building served the community for thirty-seven years, but in 1905, it was remodeled extensively. Architect O. E. Sprouce directed the work. He altered the exterior appearance of the building by raising the height of the dome twenty feet and changing the slope of the roof. He also added a dome to the rounded portico over the main entrance. The rounded portico is reminiscent of the 1826 St. Louis Courthouse, and the dome is similar to the dome on the portico on the 1837 Missouri State Capitol.

The 138-year-old courthouse continues to serve the Moniteau County citizens every day. The building is listed on the National Register of Historic Places.

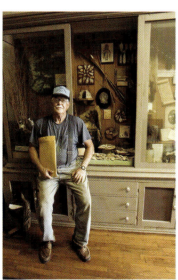

Monroe County

Organized: January 6, 1831 | County Seat: Paris | Architect: William W. Rose and David B. Peterson

In 1831, the county paid one hundred dollars for land to use as the county square and then appropriated three thousand dollars to build the county's first courthouse, a neatly finished, foursquare-style, two-story, brick building. That courthouse burned in December 1861, and the county was without one for the duration of the Civil War. A replacement courthouse was built in 1867. That courthouse was razed in 1912 to make way for the current courthouse.

After three unsuccessful bond elections, voters agreed in 1911 to build themselves a replacement courthouse. In 1912, county officials awarded the construction contract for a bid of $83,450. Monroe County's current courthouse is notable as the last Missouri courthouse built with a dome.

Montgomery County

Organized: December 14, 1818 | County Seat: Montgomery City | Architect: Ernest T. Friton

The process of selecting Montgomery City as the county seat was a long and winding road. In 1819, officials picked Pinckney, a town on the Missouri River, as the county seat. The location was inconvenient, however, and in 1824, the county seat was moved to Lewiston.

In 1834, the legislature separated Warren County from Montgomery County, and the county seat was moved once again, this time to Danville. Danville citizens built a temporary courthouse on the square and in 1865 replaced that building with a new courthouse.

Railroads had a part to play in Montgomery County's county seat selection process too. The North Missouri Railroad reached Montgomery City in 1857, and the town prospered and became the premier trading center for the county. The townspeople began to have aspirations for being named as the county seat, and in 1889, Montgomery City lobbied successfully to have circuit and probate court cases heard in the city. Montgomery City built a new courthouse, making a gift of the new building to the county. Support for moving the county seat to Montgomery City increased daily.

Danville resisted the pressure to have the county seat moved to Montgomery City, but when its courthouse burned in 1901, the die was cast. Those who supported Danville to remain as the county seat realized they did not have the countywide support they would need to rebuild their courthouse, and so the county seat was transferred to Montgomery City.

Montgomery City's 1889 courthouse served the county until 1953 when it was condemned, and that same year, the voters authorized four hundred thousand dollars in bonds to build a new building. The cornerstone ceremony for the new courthouse was held in April 1954, and the present Montgomery County Courthouse was completed in 1955.

Top: The 1953 Montgomery County Courthouse was designed by St. Louis architect Ernest T. Friton, who also designed the Dunklin County Courthouse in 1940.

Bottom: Montgomery County's county seat has been located in four different communities around the county, and six different buildings have served as the county's courthouse. (From: Montgomery County Collection. Artist: Doris Morrow, 1976)

Morgan County

Organized: January 5, 1833 | County Seat: Versailles | Architect: William F. Schrage

Top: The 1889 Morgan County Courthouse is similar in design to several other courthouses designed by the same architect, including Howard County (1887), Laclede County (1894), and Ripley County (1898).

Bottom: An upside-down brick is near one of the building's drainpipes.

In 1836, Morgan County's first courthouse in the frontier town of Versailles was a log building that was purchased and reconstructed on the square. It remained there in service until 1843, when it was removed in favor of a more permanent building. The county's second courthouse, built in 1844, was a rectangular, two-story, brick building. After more than forty years of continuous use, the voters agreed to build a third courthouse, but in 1887, while the new building was under construction, the old building was destroyed by fire.

It took a judge's ruling in 1889 to clear the way for construction to proceed on the county's present courthouse in Versailles. A court case developed when the courthouse bond issue election created a major question about the interpretation of a state statute. One group of citizens argued that the two-thirds majority, which the law required, applied to the total number of eligible voters in the county. Another group of voters claimed that a two-thirds majority of those who actually voted in the election was sufficient. The judge sided with those who thought that two-thirds of actual voters settled the issue.

After the legal challenge was resolved, the county could issue the bonds that had been passed by the voters, and construction of the present courthouse went forward. Convicts made the bricks used for this courthouse, and one of the convicts secretly engraved the name of the judge who convicted him into one of the bricks. During construction, the brick was placed upside down in the wall near one of the entrances to the door.

A lighting strike damaged the tower, reducing its height by half; otherwise, the building retains its original design. The still hard-at-work courthouse is on the National Register of Historic Places.

New Madrid County

Organized: October 1, 1812 | County Seat: New Madrid | Architect: H. G. Clymer

Officials formally organized the New Madrid County as a political entity in 1812, and the established town of New Madrid was chosen as the county seat. However, between 1814 and 1822, the court moved to several different towns near the present-day location of Sikeston. Due to the aftershocks of the 1811 earthquake and repeated flooding of the Mississippi River, the county court was temporarily moved inland, away from the river.

In 1822, the county court returned to New Madrid. The new courthouse constructed there, like all of the buildings in New Madrid, was of frame construction to better withstand the after-shocks that played havoc with the more rigid brick and stone buildings. In 1854, the county built a replacement courthouse, but this building

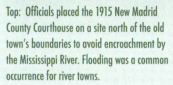

Top: Officials placed the 1915 New Madrid County Courthouse on a site north of the old town's boundaries to avoid encroachment by the Mississippi River. Flooding was a common occurrence for river towns.

Bottom left: A skylight was constructed over the courthouse's central rotunda to brighten the interior. The stained glass features interlacing vines with red roses and stylized stems and leaves that are framed and accented by tortoiseshell-colored glass.

Bottom right: Southern style mansions, magnolia trees, cotton fields, and "Ol Man River" rolling past New Madrid's doorstep remind Missourians that the state has deep roots in the antebellum South. The Hunter-Dawson mansion was built in 1859.

had to be moved three times during the next twenty years to flee the encroaching river.

In 1875, determined to confound the Mississippi River once and for all, officials selected a new site on high ground for New Madrid's third courthouse. The building stayed dry, but was destroyed by fire in 1905. County business was conducted at rental offices around the town during the next decade.

In 1915, while all of Europe was embroiled in World War I, county officials made plans for construction of the present courthouse and purchased a site that was outside of New Madrid's city limits at that time. The voters passed a fifty thousand dollar bond issue, but additional public funds and private donations were needed to complete the task, which amounted to about one hundred thousand dollars. The cornerstone had been laid in 1915, but the work took longer than expected, because America was gearing up to enter the war in 1917 and there was a shortage of workers. The project was completed in January 1919. This courthouse continues to serve the people of New Madrid County.

Newton County

Organized: December 31, 1838 | County Seat: Neosho |
Architect: Neal C. Davis

Newton County built four courthouses during the nineteenth century. In 1840, the court constructed a hand-hewn log building, and it replaced that structure in 1847 with a foursquare building. That courthouse was destroyed by Civil War action, and the square was converted for use as a park.

In 1867, the court erected a frame building on a lot purchased north of the old square. That building stood until 1878, when it was razed to make way for the fourth nineteenth-century courthouse, which featured a distinctive roof and tower design. The tower's dome was removed during the 1920s, and the entire building was razed in 1935 to make way for the present courthouse.

Plans for the new courthouse were approved in 1935, and funding was provided by a Work Projects Administration grant. Construction began in spring of 1936, and that summer, Harry S. Truman, then the junior senator from Missouri and grand steward of the Masonic Grand Lodge of Missouri, was the featured speaker at the building's dedication ceremony. County officials accepted the completed building in 1937, and it remains in service today.

Top: Five murals cover the corridor walls in the Newton County Courthouse. Historic murals are a growing trend at courthouses in Missouri. (From: Newton CountyCollection. Artists: Billie Gofourth-Stewart and Julie Lankford Olds, 1996)

Middle: Kay Baum, Newton County Clerk, holds a photo of the 1877–1935 Newton County Courthouse. Portions of the ornate tower were removed around 1920, and the entire structure was razed in 1935 to make way for the present courthouse.

Bottom: The 1936 Newton County Courthouse measures about 112 by 90 feet. General offices are on the first floor, and the circuit court is on the second floor.

Nodaway County

Organized: February 14, 1845 | County Seat: Maryville | Architects: Edmond J. Eckel and George R. Mann

Early courts in Nodaway County met in schoolhouses, private homes, and other available meeting spaces. In 1846, the court ordered construction to begin on the county's first courthouse, a two-room log building, but the court was discontented over the slow progress of the casual contractor who took over a year to build the structure.

The county's second courthouse, a foursquare building, was started in 1853 and ready for occupancy in 1855. Apparently the allocation of space in the new building was not to everyone's satisfaction, and in 1869, the courtroom on the first floor was moved to the second floor and the offices on the second floor were relocated to the first. These moves satisfied all concerned, until the building was razed in 1881 to make way for construction of the current courthouse.

The voters authorized the present courthouse and a jail in 1881. After 125 years, the courthouse's rakishly thin, tall clock tower continues to please the eye. This building is the work of two of the finest architects who designed courthouses and public buildings in Missouri. It is listed on the National Register of Historic Places.

Top: The 1881 Nodaway County Courthouse is one of many buildings in northwest Missouri designed by the St. Joseph firm of Eckel and Mann.

Middle: Isaac Charles Parker was St. Joseph's city attorney before being elected as circuit judge in Nodaway County during the 1860s. His picture hangs today in the Nodaway County Courthouse, along with all of the other judges who have presided in the Twelfth Missouri Circuit Court. In 1875, President Grant appointed Parker as judge of the district court at Fort Smith, Arkansas, with a mandate to clean up the Oklahoma Territory. During Judge Parker's twenty-one years on the federal bench, he tried 13,490 cases, 344 of which were capital crimes. Of the 160 (156 men and 4 women) that Parker sentenced to death by hanging, 79 went to the gallows. The rest escaped the rope by dying in jail, successfully appealing their sentences, or by being pardoned.

Bottom: The Nodaway County Commission, Bob Westfall (left), Lester Keith, and Bob Stiens listen to a request from Gary Ecker, mayor of the town of Elmo. Kevin Rosenbohm, local resident, observes.

Oregon County

Organized: February 14, 1845 |
County Seat: Alton | Architect:
Earl Hawkins

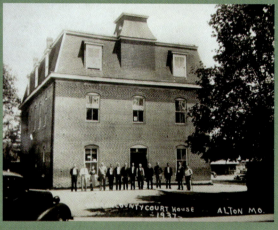

Oregon's first county seat was at
Thomasville, a town near the Eleven-Point
River. In 1847, the court constructed a
twenty-foot-square, two-story, log courthouse, but this building was abandoned
in 1860 when the county seat was moved to Alton. The county built a replacement courthouse
in Alton, a foursquare-style building that was completed in 1861 but destroyed by fire in 1863
during a civil war incident..

In 1870, the people cleared off the foundation of the burned building and constructed a
replacement courthouse of similar size and room layout on the same site. In 1903, that courthouse was expanded into a rectangular shape and then covered with a mansard roof, adding a
third floor to the building.

The availability of Work Projects Administration grant money during the 1930s encouraged
Oregon County voters to authorize construction of the current courthouse. The WPA supplied three-fourths of the funds, and Oregon County provided the remaining one quarter for
the new courthouse. The building was dedicated in 1942 and continues to serve the people of
Oregon County.

Top: Missouri red granite was used on the 1939
Oregon County Courthouse. Local stone had
been requested, but granite from Iron County
quarries was more economical.

Bottom: In 1937, Oregon County officials gather
at the courthouse. The 1871 building was
remodeled in 1904 and razed in 1939. (From:
Oregon County Collection)

Osage County

Organized: January 29, 1841 | County Seat: Linn | Architect: Henry H. Hohenschild

Top: Highway 50 passes directly in front of the 1923 Osage County Courthouse. Widening of the road over the years has forced the county to place its monuments on the roadside opposite from the courthouse.

Bottom: The 1872 courthouse was remodeled in 1881 after being damaged by fire. The most important exterior alteration during the rebuilding was the installation of a dome to replace the square belfry—still in place in this painting. (From: Osage County Collection. Artist: Butch Herndon, 1988)

After meeting in various homes around the county for several years, the court decided to build the county's first courthouse. A contract was awarded in August 1843, and work began on the two-story, brick building early in 1844. A stone wall was built around the yard in 1854, and a fence was added in 1860, probably to keep livestock from gazing on the grass.

A new courthouse was authorized in 1872, and the existing courthouse was sold in 1874 for scrap, about the time that the replacement building was ready for occupancy.

Six years later, in 1880, the new courthouse was partially damaged by a fire. During the building's repair, the court renovated the interior and replaced the belfry with a taller, octagonal dome. Architects Joseph B. Goesse and Frederick J. Rimmers, from St. Louis, supervised the renovation. After these improvements were made, the courtroom was considered to be one of the best furnished and well-planned in Missouri. Fire destroyed the building completely in 1922.

In 1923, work began on the current courthouse. County finances were tight, so the plan for a replacement courthouse entailed incorporating the existing foundations and walls in the new building. The building was completed in October of 1925 and continues to serve the people of Osage County.

Ozark County

Organized: January 29, 1841 | County Seat: Gainesville | Architect: Earl Hawkins

The budget for the 1939 Ozark County Courthouse was set at $35,000, but early bids exceeded that amount. Architect Earl Hawkins revised his plans to enable a winning bid of $34,950.

When Ozark County was chartered in 1841, its boundaries included land that was later used to create Douglas County. Rockbridge, a town that was centrally located before the boundary lines were redrawn, was selected as the county seat, and a courthouse was built there. Fire destroyed the building in 1859, but since the legislature had separated Douglas County from Ozark County several years earlier, the Rockbridge site was no longer geographically suitable as the Ozark County Seat.

In 1860, the county court established its new county seat at Gainesville and constructed a courthouse in that town. As was often the case throughout the Civil War, that building was destroyed by fire in 1864. A decade passed before a replacement courthouse was built, and it served until it was destroyed by fire in 1934.

The 1873 courthouse, a two-story, frame building, served the county until it was destroyed by fire in 1934. The court purchased an unused church building as temporary quarters, but it burned as well in 1937. County offices functioned from rented office spaces around the square.

In 1938, the citizens rallied to vote in favor of a bond issue for a replacement courthouse. A Work Projects Administration grant was awarded to cover 45 percent of the anticipated cost, and a construction contract was signed in March 1939. Work on the building moved swiftly, and the builder completed the job in November 1939. The building still serves the people of Ozark County.

Pemiscot County

Organized: February 19, 1851 | County Seat: Caruthersville | Architect: Henry H. Hohenschild

Pemiscot County's first three courthouses were built in Gayoso, a town located about three miles upstream on the Mississippi River from present-day Caruthersville. In 1854, the county built its first Gayoso courthouse, and it served until 1873. The second, built that same year, burned in 1882.

The county received a second allocation from the state to build its third courthouse, and a two-story, frame building was constructed in 1883 for about four thousand dollars. Unfortunately, even with a new courthouse, the current was running hard against Gayoso's continuing tenure as the county seat. Floods plagued the town, and in 1899, the citizens petitioned to have the county seat moved to Caruthersville.

In 1899, Caruthersville was the site selected, and residents donated sufficient land to establish a courthouse square in the center of the town. The county's fourth courthouse, a two-story, white, frame building with a hip roof, was ready for occupancy that same year. That courthouse was retired in 1924 and moved to the northwest corner of the square to make way for the current courthouse.

Work began in 1924 on both the present courthouse and a school. The duel project was a cost-saving move and a means of assuring the attention of the architect who designed both buildings. In an unusual move, the contractor's bid for the projects was reduced because the cost of materials had declined between the time bids were requested and the actual starting date of construction. Work was completed in the fall of 1925.

The building was renovated in 1975 and remains the seat of justice for Pemiscot County.

The 1924 Pemiscot County Courthouse design is similar to Scott County's 1911 courthouse. Both buildings were designed by prolific architect Henry H. Hohenschild.

Perry County

Organized: November 16, 1820 | County
Seat: Perryville | Architect: J. W. Gaddis

Early court officials conducted business sessions in a private home, a hewn-log structure that was used into the twentieth century for other purposes. In 1825, plans were made to build a courthouse, and the county sold fifty-five lots from property donated to the county to pay for the construction costs. The building was completed in 1826 and served the community for the next thirty years, but by 1859, it was apparent that that building was no longer large enough to accommodate the needs of the fast growing county. The replacement courthouse was completed in 1861 and continued in use until the turn of the century, when it was considered beyond repair.

Perry County voters approved a bond issue for the present courthouse in September 1903. Construction of the new building began in February 1904. The building's construction site was next to the existing courthouse. After the replacement courthouse was completed later that same year, the old and new courthouses stood side by side for a time. Soon, the old courthouse building was dismantled and removed from the square.

The 1904 Perry County Courthouse retains its original appearance and remains in use today.

The 1923 Pettis County Courthouse stands in the heart of Sedalia's Historic Business District. It was built with an exterior of Bedford stone, and the lobbies are lined with Minnesota marble.

Pettis County

Organized: January 16, 1833 | County Seat: Sedalia | Architect: W. E. Hulse

Officials moved the county seat's location twice before selecting Sedalia in 1865. In the years between 1833 and 1837, the court met at a private home in St. Helena, and in 1837, the county seat was moved next to Georgetown. The sum of four thousand dollars was allocated by the county to build a foursquare style courthouse in that community. That courthouse building survived until it was destroyed by fire in 1920, but the county seat had already been moved to Sedalia in 1865.

Sedalia's courthouse, constructed in 1865, was a large, frame building with office space rented to attorneys—a standard practice of the day. In 1882, several attorneys who maintained offices in the courthouse became put-out with what they considered to be the run-down condition of the facility. They decided to mount a campaign to build a new courthouse, and they appealed to civil pride by pointing out that other neighboring counties were upgrading their courthouses to showcase prosperity and progress and that Pettis County's decaying courthouse made the town look dowdy and outdated. Not to be out done by other counties, in December

1883, the public overwhelmingly approved a one hundred thousand dollar bond issue for construction of a new courthouse.

In 1884, the new courthouse was completed. There does not seem to be a record of what accommodations, if any, were made for lawyers in the new building, and, unfortunately, the building was destroyed by fire in 1920.

In 1923, after rejecting three previous appeals, voters approved a bond issue for the current courthouse, but the construction was not without criticism. For starters, the court hired an out-of-state architect before appointing a building committee or naming a construction superintendent. This unorthodox move raised a question as to whether or not the court followed legal procedure. Once that hurdle was cleared, the architect was accused of kowtowing to the court's wishes and placing the circuit court and some county offices on the more inconvenient second and third floors of the three-story building.

Lady Justice was saved from the fire that consumed the 1884 courthouse in 1920. The restored painting now resides in the third-floor circuit courtroom above the judge's bench. (From: Pettis County Collection. Artist: Charles Holloway)

The building was dedicated in May 1925, and over time, the discontent subsided. The courthouse continues to serve as the seat of justice for Pettis County.

Top: The 1994 Phelps County Courthouse was dedicated May 22, 1994. The late Governor Mel Carnahan was the speaker at the ceremony.

Bottom left: The 1859–2004 Phelps County Courthouse is located several hundred yards east of the new courthouse. The 147-year-old building was built for a cost of $7,975, but the court deducted $2,000 for unsatisfactory workmanship. The bricks used to build the courthouse were reported to be the first bricks made in Rolla.

Bottom middle: The Dillon House, a hewn-log building that was the site of early county court meetings, was moved to the courthouse square in 1969. It serves as a museum and is maintained by the Phelps County Historical Society.

Bottom right: Betty and Roy Olley (left) from Lincoln, England, tour the Dillon House with Diane Henke, curator of the Phelps County Historical Society. The cupboard served as the community's post office and is located in the general store portion of the building. The Olleys have made twelve visits to America.

Phelps County

Organized: November 13, 1857 | County Seat: Rolla | Architect: Stack and Associates

The state legislature created Phelps County in 1857 by decreasing the size of three surrounding counties—Crawford, Pulaski, and Maries. Rolla, the county seat for the new county, was created by virtue of its central geographic location and was little more than a clearing in the wilderness surrounded by trees and isolated from other communities.

The first county court convened on November 25, 1857, in John Dillon's cabin located northeast of present day Rolla. Urgent court business during those early sessions included road construction to provide access to other communities around the state and to encourage settlers to travel into the area.

In 1859, the county built its first courthouse, a 45-by-65-foot brick building with a cupola. Union troops used the building as a base of operations during the Civil War, and later, it served as a hospital for the duration of the strife. In 1881, the building was enlarged, and the cupola was removed sometime in the 1940s.

Since its retirement in 1994 as the county courthouse, the building continues its useful life as the home of the Phelps County Museum. The City of Rolla's Municipal Court also hears cases on scheduled days each week in the second-floor courtroom.

In 1994, county offices transferred to the current Phelps County Courthouse.

Pike County

Organized: December 14, 1818 |
County Seat: Bowling Green | Architect:
Henry H. Hohenschild

Louisiana, a town on the Mississippi River, was Pike County's first county seat. In 1819, the court met in a small building—the first brick building constructed in the county—that continued to serve the county until 1824, even though the county seat had been moved to the centrally located town of Bowling Green several years earlier.

In 1823, a hewn-log building was built to serve as a temporary courthouse in Bowling Green. It was replaced in 1829 by a second, temporary building, albeit of brick construction. In 1843, county officials decided to build what was to be the county's first permanent courthouse building. After twenty years, in 1864, that courthouse was destroyed by fire. The county's next courthouse, built in 1865, also burned in 1915.

In 1915, the county approved a bond issue to build two courthouses—one in Bowling Green and another in Louisiana—but the election was challenged due to vague language on the ballot. The Missouri Supreme Court agreed that the language was unclear, and the election was overturned. In 1916, the issue was rewritten and placed once again before the voters, but with a different explanation of their choices, the electorate approved the Bowling Green Courthouse and rejected building a second courthouse in Louisiana.

Work began in 1917 on Bowling Green's courthouse, and the building was occupied in 1919. The courthouse continues to serve as the Pike County seat of justice.

Top: The statue on the lawn of the Pike County Courthouse honors Bowling Green's most famous son, Camp Clark, speaker of the House (1911–19), presidential candidate (1912), and long-serving congressman from Pike County.

Middle: Pike County deputy court clerks, Kathy Kurz (left) and Nadine Lawson, appropriated the associate courtroom and used seats and tabletops for file storage while their office space was being renovated.

Bottom: Pike County Clerk Bob Kirkpatrick poses beside the colorful Pike County seal that is mounted on a wall behind the judge's bench in the courthouse's second-story circuit courtroom.

Platte County

Organized: December 31, 1838 | County Seat: Platte City | Architect: Peter McDuff

Top: The triple-arched entry is a feature of the 1866 Platte County Courthouse. The building was designed by a Scottish immigrant, Peter McDuff, who also designed courthouses for Clinton (1858) and Clay Counties (1859).

Bottom left: Don Doolen, facilities manager, inspects an original roof timber that supports the core building's 140-year-old roof. This section of the attic is immediately above the circuit courtroom.

Bottom right: Zinc ceiling tiles were discovered during a courthouse renovation in 2000. Several of the stamped tiles were restored to their original color and placed on display in the courthouse lobby.

In 1838, Platte County commissioners purchased a log building to use as their first courthouse. They used this rough building for almost two years before ordering the construction of a 50-foot-square brick, two-story courthouse in 1840. Completed in 1842, that building did not survive the Civil War.

In 1864, construction began on the current courthouse, and it was ready for occupancy in 1867. The original building measured 80 by 100 feet. Several additions have expanded the size of the building. The building continues to serve the people of Platte County.

The courthouse is listed on the National Register of Historic Places.

Polk County

Organized: January 5, 1835 | County Seat: Bolivar | Architect: Robert G. Kirsch

In 1835, William Jamison purchased land from the federal government—the largest real estate agency of that time. He donated part of this land to create Bolivar, the county seat. Several years later, in 1837, the court appropriated $125 to build a temporary courthouse on its new county square. The building served its purpose until 1842 and was then sold to the highest bidder.

In 1839, planning was underway to construct a permanent courthouse. By 1841, shortly before the court abandoned its temporary building, the foursquare-style building was almost complete. Although this courthouse survived the Civil War, accidental fire, arson, and the various other calamities that afflicted almost all of Missouri's nineteenth-century courthouses, it had to be vacated in 1905 for safety reasons.

The voters authorized a bond issue that same year to build the current courthouse. In May 1906, the Masonic Lodge conducted a cornerstone ceremony, and the building was completed in November 1907. The architect, Robert O. Kirsch, had used his popular design to build three other Missouri courthouses—Adair (1898), Carroll (1901), and Vernon (1906).

Recycling a courthouse design was not unusual because it was not practical to create an entirely new design for each building competition. If the building committee selected a design that had been used to build another courthouse, it modified the plan by changing the tower or specified brick instead of stone veneer to make its building unique.

Top: If you want someone to help, ask a county official. Judy Mackey, Polk County Treasurer, sells Polk County T-shirts to support the county's annual American Cancer Society's Relay for Life event.

Middle: Steve Bruce, Polk County Sheriff (left), Billy Dryer, Associate Commissioner, and Roy Harms, Presiding Commissioner, take turns examining a machine gun used by Pretty Boy Floyd, a 1930s-era bank robber. In 1933, Polk County Sheriff Jack Killingsworth was captured and held hostage by Floyd, narrowly escaping with his life. At some point during those adventures, the machine gun ended up in the county's weapons locker.

Bottom: The 1906 Polk County Courthouse was one of the last Romanesque-design courthouses to be built in Missouri. The contract for construction of the building was awarded to a St. Louis firm for a bid of $41,950.

Pulaski County

Organized: January 19, 1833 | County Seat: Waynesville | Architect: Warren and Goodin Inc.

Missouri has had two counties named Pulaski. The first Pulaski County was organized in 1818 but was not located within the boundaries of the present Pulaski County; nor did it survive the frequent reconfiguration of larger counties into smaller units during Missouri's early expansion years.

In 1833, the legislature organized a second Pulaski County, but that version of the county also experienced many boundary changes before assuming its present shape in 1859.

The county built its first courthouse in 1840. The hewn-log structure was located near the present-day western border of Phelps County, on the Little Piney River. In 1843, the county moved the county seat to Waynesville, and the county officials ordered construction of their first permanent courthouse there. That building suffered severe damage during the Civil War, but it remained in use until 1872, when it was considered unsafe and beyond repair.

The state appropriated two thousand dollars in war damages because of damages to the courthouse during the Civil War, and those funds, along with a six thousand dollar bond issue, went toward a new courthouse that was erected in 1873. That courthouse was destroyed by fire in 1903.

The 1903–89 courthouse features a tower with an observation deck and an octagonal-shaped addition. That Pulaski County Courthouse is listed on the National Register of Historic Places. In 1989, the county built a replacement courthouse next door to the old courthouse.

Top: The modern design of the 1989 Pulaski County Courthouse provides a clear contrast to its predecessor 1903 building that stands next door.

Bottom left: Diana Linnenbringer, Pulaski County Clerk, looks at the 1874 registry of people admitted to the county farm or almshouse. The farm provided shelter and food for those with no other means of support. A list of rules governed daily life at the poor farm. Orders included: inmates should not be in their rooms during daylight hours, mandatory weekly baths, and no lights after eight o'clock at night.

Bottom right: The 1903–89 Pulaski County Courthouse has been preserved and serves as an excellent example of an early twentieth-century Missouri courthouse. The building is maintained by the Pulaski County Historical Society and houses a period museum.

Top: The 1923 courthouse facade is Carthage limestone, a popular building material from Jasper County that is hard enough to be polished like marble and considered suitable for either exterior or interior use.

Putnam County

Organized: February 28, 1845 | County Seat: Unionville | Architect: J. G. Braecklein

Between 1845 and 1851, Putnam County had three county seats, or perhaps four. In 1845, Putnamville was selected, and in 1848, officials moved the seat of government to Winchester. In 1851, it was moved again to the town of Fairplay, later renamed Hartford. The total number of moves is unclear, because in 1847 although the court ordered a move to Calhoun, the order may not have been executed, and the county seat was moved directly to Winchester. The shifting of a county seat from one location to another was not an uncommon event

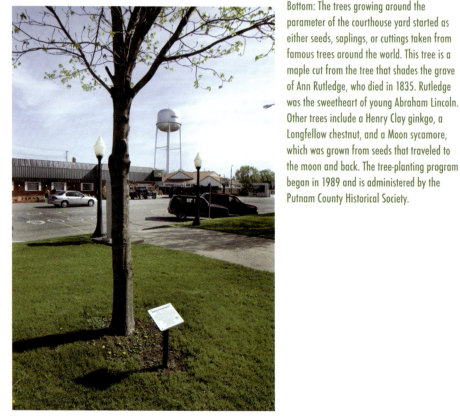

Bottom: The trees growing around the parameter of the courthouse yard started as either seeds, saplings, or cuttings taken from famous trees around the world. This tree is a maple cut from the tree that shades the grave of Ann Rutledge, who died in 1835. Rutledge was the sweetheart of young Abraham Lincoln. Other trees include a Henry Clay ginkgo, a Longfellow chestnut, and a Moon sycamore, which was grown from seeds that traveled to the moon and back. The tree-planting program began in 1989 and is administered by the Putnam County Historical Society.

during the early settlement days in pioneer Missouri. Young settlements were still provisional then, and there had been little investment made in constructing permanent county buildings, such as a courthouse or jail. The fact that many of Missouri's early counties were still being divided by the legislature into smaller units—a process that shifted the geographical centers of the resulting new counties—also complicated the question of where to locate the county seat.

In 1851, Putnam and Dodge, two adjoining Missouri counties, both had their boundaries reduced when the U.S. Supreme Court resolved the Missouri–Iowa border dispute by awarding acreage to Iowa. Both counties were left with less than the minimum territory required by state law for county organization, so in1853, the legislature disbanded Dodge County and attached that land to Putnam. Accordingly, in 1854, officials relocated the Putnam County Seat once again to the geographic center of the newly configured county. The new county seat was named Harmony—optimistically signaling reconciliation between the citizens of Putnam and the residents of defunct Dodge County—but the name was changed to Unionville in 1855.

Unionville's first courthouse was a temporary structure, a two-story, log building with a brick chimney and stone foundation, and it was used from 1854 to 1858. A permanent courthouse was built in 1857. It was a foursquare-style building with a square belfry that was capped with a dome and weathervane. The second-floor courtroom was condemned and unused during the 1880s, and the building was sold and removed from the square in 1890. More than thirty years would pass before the county would build another courthouse.

In 1923, a surge of public pride compelled citizens to press for an election to authorize construction of a new courthouse. Virtually all Missouri counties had courthouses, and many citizens of Putnam County were embarrassed to be without one. A $150,000 bond election passed in June 1923, and when victory was announced, people danced in the street in celebration. Contracts were issued in 1923. The building was dedicated in November 1924, but disagreements over the quality of some of the workmanship delayed final acceptance of the courthouse until January 1925. The building is still used as Putnam County's courthouse.

Sue Ann Varner, county clerk, holds portraits of several of the county's early courthouses. The log building was used from 1854 to 1858, and the foursquare-style courthouse remained in use from 1857 to 1890. (Putnam County Collection. Artist: Will E. Livezey, 1925)

Ralls County

Organized: November 16, 1820 | County Seat: New London | Architect: Henry C. Wellman

In the eighteenth century, French trappers were drawn to the Salt River region because of the plentiful brine springs needed for making salt and to trade with the Native American tribes living in the area. English-speaking settlers who arrived in the area after the Louisiana Purchase were more interested in cultivating the rich farmland. As Indians ceded their hunting territories for land farther west, the settlers proceeded to build a rich agricultural economy that continues to flourish to this day.

New London, the town that became the county seat, was founded in 1819—a year prior to the legislature granting Ralls County the right to formally organize. In 1822, the county constructed its first courthouse in New London. It was a two-story, log building with a jail and dungeon on the first floor. That structure remained in service until 1835, when the court replaced it with a foursquare-style building that had a courtroom on the first floor. In 1858, that courthouse was sold and removed from the square.

Having formed a building committee in 1857 to make recommendations for a new courthouse, the court accepted the committee's plan in 1858 to build a Temple Front courthouse. The Ralls County building, finished in 1859, is one of two Greek-Revival courthouses still in service in the state of Missouri. The other is the Lafayette County Courthouse, built in 1847.

Top: The courthouse was designed by Henry C. Wellman, county attorney and amateur architect, who consulted several handbooks on carpentry and construction techniques before submitting his plans to the county court.

Middle: Glenn Shreve, project superintendent for a Troy contracting firm, plumbs a new door casing for the courthouse. The restoration project began in spring of 2005, and it was completed in mid-2006.

Bottom: Ernest E. Duckworth, county clerk, along with other county officers, conducts county business from a desk inside a warehouse during the renovation period. The courthouse staff returned to their offices in mid-2006.

In 1938, the county received a Work Projects Administration grant to build a two-story addition at the rear of the building. The stone used for the addition came from the abutments and middle pier of an old bridge over the Salt River, and the stone was a close match for the locally quarried limestone that was used to build the original building.

In 2005, the court ordered a renovation of the interior of the courthouse. While the building was closed for repairs, the furniture and records were stored, and the staff conducted business from a nearby temporary facility. In 2006, the restoration work was completed, and the 1858 courthouse continues to serve the people of Ralls County as their seat of justice. The building is listed on the National Register of Historic Places.

Randolph County

Organized: January 22, 1829 | County Seat: Huntsville | Architect: James McGrath

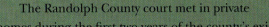

The Randolph County court met in private homes during the first two years of the county's existence. The court held sessions in a foursquare courthouse in the years between 1831 and 1858, and a replacement courthouse was erected in 1858. By 1876, however, that building was considered unsafe and the question of a bond issue for building a new courthouse was placed on the ballot.

The bond issue was decisively defeated—a reflection of a widespread sentiment that it was not a good time to spend money on a new courthouse in Huntsville, especially since there was a movement afoot to move the county seat to Moberly. Rather than put the issue before the voters a second time, the court chose to use county funds to remodel the old building—a move that did not require voter approval—and work on the courthouse was completed in 1877.

The rivalry between Huntsville and Moberly over the location of the county seat may have played a part in the fire that destroyed the Huntsville seat of justice on August 12, 1882. As flames engulfed the Huntsville Courthouse, an eyewitness reported seeing a figure fleeing the building, and arson was suspected. Soon afterwards, the issue of moving the county seat was put to the voters. Moberly received a majority but did not garner the two-thirds votes required by state law. Whether or not the two events were related remains open to conjecture, but in any case, Huntsville began construction on its third courthouse in December 1882, using a design by architect James McGrath.

McGrath's courthouse was completed in 1884. It was a two-story, brick building with a tower. Sometime before 1910, however, most of the tower was removed; and in 1955, following a fire that destroyed the second floor, the courthouse was rebuilt as a one-story building. The county continues to use this building and maintains a satellite courthouse in Moberly.

Top far right: This pencil sketch shows James McGrath's original design for the 1882 courthouse. (From: Randolph County collection, City Bank & Trust Company: Moberly Heritage Collection. Artist: James Burkhart)

Top: Shiela Miller (left), collector of revenue, and Neta Crutchfield, deputy collector, check a ledger at the doorway to one of the county's fire-resistant vaults.

Middle: This satellite courthouse is located in Moberly. Located several miles east of Huntsville, Moberly is the largest community in the county.

Bottom: Rebuilt as a one-story building following a fire in 1955, the 1882 courthouse no longer reflects architect James McGrath's original design.

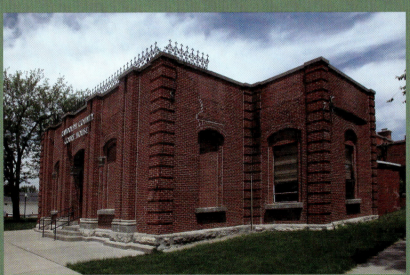

Ray County

Organized: November 16, 1820 | County Seat: Richmond | Architect: Warren Roberts

Ray County was one of the counties created from Howard County, a mega-county that eventually spawned twenty-nine separate counties and parts of nine others. Organization of the new county must have been a traumatic event, however, because six years passed before the commissioners could agree on a location for the county seat. Richmond was finally selected and a hewn-log building became the county's first courthouse in 1829.

In 1856, a second courthouse was constructed. The building's Greek-Revival design was inspired by the Temple Front Courthouse in neighboring Lafayette County. In 1878, a storm tore off the tin-covered roof and weakened the cupola. This courthouse served the county for nearly sixty years, and in 1914, the building was sold to the United Mine Workers Union and was moved to a different location.

In 1913, to meet the needs of an expanding community, the voters approved a bond issue of one hundred thousand dollars for construction of a new courthouse. Architect R. Warren Roberts designed the building. He was also the architect for nearby Livingston County's 1913 courthouse. The present courthouse was completed in November 1915. Features on the courthouse lawn include metal columns from the interior of the 1856 building and a statue, by sculptor F. C. Hibbard, that honors Alexander W. Doniphan. Colonel Doniphan lived in Richmond for nineteen years and led the First Regiment Missouri Mounted Volunteers on their famed 1846–47 self-sustained expedition to Mexico during the Mexican War. The Ray County Courthouse is listed on the National Register of Historic Places.

Top: The 1914 Ray County Courthouse is similar in design to the 1913 courthouse built in nearby Livingston County. The Ray County Courthouse Building Committee visited with architect R. Warren Roberts at the courthouse construction site in Chillicothe before offering him the Ray County commission.

Bottom: The 1856–1914 Ray County Courthouse was purchased and moved to make way for the present courthouse. It was razed in the 1960s. (From: Ray County Collection. Photograph donated by John Crouch)

Reynolds County

Organized: February 25, 1845 | County Seat: Centerville | Architect: Unknown

The town of Lesterville was the county seat for the first twenty years of Reynolds County's organized existence. In 1846, the court built a small log courthouse, but fire consumed the building and all records in 1862.

The court met in private homes until the end of the Civil War. In 1865, the county seat was moved to Centerville, and officials ordered construction of a small, log courthouse. Six years later, that building was also destroyed by fire. The day after the fire, the commissioners met amongst the debris and authorized ten thousand dollars for construction of a new courthouse.

The present courthouse, a two-story, rectangular, brick building was completed in 1872. The original plans called for a dome, but it was never built. During the 1930s, when the Work Projects Administration offered assistance to counties in Missouri to build or repair public buildings, Reynolds County had to decline because it could not financially support its share of the expense. In 1981, an addition was built at the rear of the building to house the sheriff's office and jail. Otherwise, the building is true to its 135-year-old design. This is one of the oldest courthouses in Missouri, and it continues to serve the people of Reynolds County.

The 1871 Reynolds County Courthouse originally measured 50 by 40 feet and cost eight thousand dollars. The county appropriated the funds to build this courthouse the morning after a fire destroyed the previous courthouse.

Ripley County

Organized: January 5, 1833 | County Seat: Doniphan | Architect: William Schrage

In 1838, Ripley County, one of Missouri's early mega-counties, still contained approximately 20 percent of the state's land mass. Within twenty years, the legislature carved new counties from Ripley's vast boundaries and shrank the county to its present size.

In 1847, Van Buren was Ripley's first county seat. At that time, Ripley County still contained land that is now Carter County, and because most of the population was in the southern half of the double-sized county, the voters decided to ignore the geographical center rule and move the county seat south, where it would be closer to the center of population. This decision led to the creation of a new town named Doniphan near the Current River. Van Buren retained its county seat status in Carter County when the legislature separated it from Ripley and made it an independent county in 1859.

In 1848, officials built a log building in Doniphan to serve as the first courthouse. Civil War hostilities destroyed the town and the courthouse. In 1871, the community erected a replacement courthouse, but fire destroyed that building in 1898.

In 1898, voters quickly authorized the sale of bonds to build the current courthouse. Completed in 1899, the building tower is located above the main entrance. The tower cap structure has been removed, and during the 1930s, a Work Projects Administration grant was used to repair weather damage to the building. Extensive remodeling in 1976 provided the building with a central heating system. The 108-year-old building is listed on the National Register of Historic Places.

Top: The 1898 Ripley County Courthouse architect, William F. Schrage, also designed similar courthouses for Morgan, Laclede, and Howard Counties, but those courthouses all featured central towers.

Bottom left: Straight-back chairs provide seating in the Ripley County circuit courtroom. The stenciling on the chairs indicates reserved seating for lawyers and police.

Bottom right: Becky York, county clerk, holds a painting of the courthouse that was donated to the county to "brighten the walls of the Clerk's office." (From: Ripley County Collection. Artist: Jerry Holland, 1995)

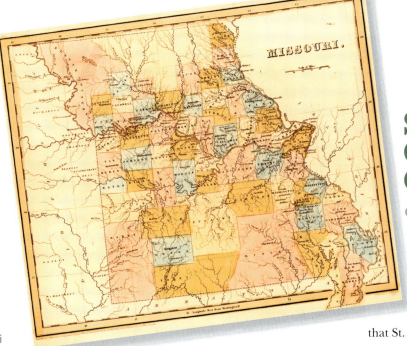

St. Charles County

Organized: October 1, 1812 | County Seat: St. Charles | Architect: Jerome B. Legg

Top: 1838 Missouri (Courtesy: Missouri Secretary of State, Missouri State Archives)

Bottom: The 1901 St. Charles County Courthouse was built on Clerks' Hill, so named because small buildings to house the county and circuit clerks' offices had been built on the site some years earlier.

Some people thought that St. Charles's proximity to St. Louis would restrict its growth, but its position on the Missouri River and the town's abundant ferry services made it the first steppingstone for travelers headed west. The increase in river traffic that followed the introduction of steam-powered boats onto the Missouri River early in the nineteenth century and the opening of the Santa Fe and Oregon Trails further ensured St. Charles' prosperity. In 1812, the territorial legislature established St. Charles County as one of the original five counties in the Missouri territory.

In 1812, the court held its sessions in rented rooms in Peck's Row, a two-story, brick building on the main street of St. Charles. Those rooms were the same accommodations the Peck brothers later rented to the first state general assembly when it met in St. Charles from 1821 to 1825.

In 1833, the county purchased a house and lot to serve as the first home for the county court. In 1846, the court began construction on the county's first permanent courthouse on that site—a one-story Temple Front building designed by architect Solomon Jenkins, who also built courthouses in Warren (1838), Scotland, and Callaway (1856) Counties. In 1849, separate fireproof clerks' offices were built near the courthouse. The courthouse continued in use until it was razed in 1903, when the court moved to a different location.

The county purchased land from the city of St. Charles for use as a new courthouse site in 1851, but county elections to approve construction of a new building failed in both 1888 and 1894. After appointing an architect in 1898—a move that had to be rescinded

Top: The portico on the 1846-1903 courthouse was supported by six columns with fluted shafts. Pilasters were placed between the windows along the sides of the building. (From: Library of Congress)

Bottom: St. Charles County's first court met in rented space at Peck's Row. Missouri's first government used the same office space in St. Charles from 1821 to 1825. (From: Missouri State Capitol. Lunette by Richard Miller)

due to the county's uncertain financial condition—the court commenced construction of the present courthouse in December 1900, using the plans that architect Jerome B. Legg had prepared in 1898. Legg designed similar courthouses for Gasconade (1898) and Mississippi (1899) Counties.

The new courthouse was occupied in April 1903, and since 1994, it has housed the offices of the county counselor, county council, director of administration, and county executive. Other county offices have been relocated to a nearby administrative building, and the law enforcement and judicial services have been moved to the Criminal Justice Center and Courts Administration Building.

St. Clair County

Organized: January 29, 1841 | County Seat: Osceola | Architect: Clifton B. Sloan

In 1842, after holding court session in homes for a year, the newly organized St. Clair County built its first courthouse—a two-story building on the town square. That building,

along with the rest of the town of Osceola, went up in flames during a Civil War raid in September 1861. Kansas troops, under the command of General James Lane, looted and burned the defenseless town. Some accounts claim the courthouse was only partially destroyed or rebuilt but then burned again in 1864 during another attack. In any event, the war left Osceola in ruins, and by 1865, the town's population had been reduced from 2,000 to 180.

In 1866, the voters approved an appropriation of fifteen thousand dollars to build a new courthouse. The replacement courthouse was built on the previous building's foundation, and the square, two-story, brick building had a sixteen-foot-tall cupola and an attached porch that was at the front of the building and supported by four two-story brick pillars. Even though the circuit court judge and most of the county office holders took space elsewhere several years earlier because of the unsafe and dilapidated condition of the facility, the building remained in service until 1908.

Several years passed after the building was abandoned before citizens approved a bond issue to build a new courthouse. The court ordered work to begin in 1916 on the current courthouse and selected plans submitted by Kansas City based architect Clifton B. Sloan. Progress on the building was slow, however, due to lawsuits stemming from a debt that the county had incurred forty years earlier in an unsuccessful railroad venture. During Missouri's railroad boom of the 1870s, St. Clair County sold bonds to build a railroad line that would tie the county to Missouri's rapidly growing railroad network. However, the company that had formed to operate the system failed and defaulted on the loan. St. Clair County was left with the debt but had no funds to reimburse the bond holders.

News of a bond election for a new courthouse alerted the bond holders that the county had recovered financially, and the heirs of the original lenders sued to have the old debts settled. Work was suspended on the partially completed building until the legal questions could be resolved, and in 1918, the voters acknowledged the county's obligation and passed a second bond issue to settle with the claimants.

After the legal problems associated with the railroad bonds were surmounted, work still proceeded slowly because of World War I, which had caused a manpower shortage and restriction of building materials. Work on the building restarted in 1919 and continued sporadically until it was completed in 1923. The St. Clair Courthouse continues to serve the county today.

Top: Construction of the 1916 St. Clair Courthouse involved a complicated history that spanned seven years. The obstacles to completion included debts from a failed railroad venture forty years earlier and restrictions of building materials caused by World War I.

Bottom: Circuit Judge William J. Roberts donated this painting to honor Wayne Scott, former St. Clair presiding commissioner. (From: St. Clair County Collection. Artist: Dan Brewer)

St. Francois County

Organized: December 19, 1821 | County Seat: Farmington | Architect: Norman B. Howard

In 1823, the county built its first courthouse—a foursquare-style building—using money made from the sale of fifty-two acres of land that had been donated to the county. To keep livestock from eating the grass, the county erected a five-foot-high plank fence around the courthouse square in 1845.

Three years later, the court ordered work to begin on a replacement courthouse—a two-story, rectangular, brick and stone building with a gable roof. The architect was Henry H. Wright, who also designed the Franklin (1847), Washington (1849), and Iron (1858) buildings. The county operating budget lacked sufficient funds to pay for the building, and the court financed the expenditure internally by borrowing eight thousand dollars from the canal and road fund. Twenty years later, in 1870, William F. Story, an architect from St. Louis, was asked to examine the building. Story warned the county that the building was in poor structural condition. In 1877, a grand jury condemned the building, but while county workers kept one eye cocked for falling plaster, they continued to use the building for business. It was not until plans were underway for a replacement building that the building was razed in 1885.

That same year, work began on the county's third courthouse, a 38-by-58-foot building designed by architect Jerome B. Legg. The new courthouse featured a mansard roof, which was a popular feature of the period. Legg used a similar design for the 1885 Ste. Genevieve County Courthouse, which is still in use. Much of the brick used to build the new courthouse was recycled from the previous courthouse as a not-uncommon cost-savings measure. By 1925, after forty years of service, this building showed signs of age. Even though it was evidentially not in the same state of crisis as the previous courthouse, the court took steps to replace it.

In 1925, voters agreed to authorize $250,000 for construction of the current courthouse. There was contention over the architect selection process, and it took eighteen ballots before the court decided on Norman B. Howard as the architect. This dissension may have contributed to a litany of complaints regarding Howard's conduct that included insinuations of fraud and criticism of his design for being too similar to the one he'd used for the 1922 Franklin County Courthouse. Furthermore, complaints over the quality of the cornerstone he provided led to cancellation of the cornerstone ceremony.

Despite these critical remarks, progress on the building continued through 1926 and 1927, until the court accepted it in September 1927. This courthouse continues to serve the people of St. Francois County.

Top: Local residents favored the use of red granite from nearby St. Francois County quarries for the 1926 courthouse, but the bidding process determined that Carthage marble and Bedford limestone would be used on the building's exterior.

Bottom: Kerry Glore, St. Francois County Treasurer, collects old office equipment. This nineteenth century stapler works exactly like its modern counterpart with the exception that a staple has to loaded each time it is used.

Ste. Genevieve County

Organized: October 1, 1812 | County Seat: Ste. Genevieve | Architect: Jerome B. Legg

Top: Architect Henry H. Wright designed the 1848–85 St. Francois Courthouse. His 1858 Iron County Courthouse is the only remaining example of his work.

Middle: Ste. Genevieve is one of Missouri's notably historic cities. The city lays claim to the largest collection of French colonial period homes in the United States. (From: Missouri State Capitol. Lunette by O. E. Berninghous, 1924)

Bottom: The 1915 annex (left) houses the Ste. Genevieve County administrative offices. The old jail immediately in front of the annex is no longer used for that purpose, and the 1885 courthouse, to the right of the jail, is used by the circuit court. The 1875 clerks' office building, on the far side of the courthouse, is similar in appearance to the jail building, but it is no longer used for that function. The tower over the annex is not part of that building; it is the belfry spire on the Ste. Genevieve Catholic Church.

The village of Ste. Genevieve was founded circa 1735 and is recognized as the first permanent European settlement west of the Mississippi. French colonial officials established a small trading post there in 1722. The station grew into a thriving village of fur traders, lead miners, farmers, and merchants. In 1812, after the Louisiana Purchase, the Missouri Territorial Legislature established Ste. Genevieve as one of the original five counties in the new American territory.

Early courts in Ste. Genevieve County met in private homes, but in 1821, a tax was levied to fund the construction of a courthouse. It was a brick building with cupola, and interior finish work was completed in 1826. The courthouse was commandeered by the military during the Civil War, and the court authorized sixteen hundred dollars to repair the building in 1865.

In 1875, two buildings were constructed in alignment with the courthouse. A fireproof clerk's office was built about thirty feet to the north of the courthouse, and a jail building was constructed about thirty feet to the south. These buildings are still in place but no longer used for their original purposes.

In 1885, the court built a new courthouse to replace the dilapidated structure from the 1820s. The court selected architect Jerome B. Legg to design the building and supervise its construction. In 1915, officials authorized construction of an extension at the rear of the courthouse building. Architect Robert Kirsch planned the extension, which now houses the county's administrative offices. The 1885 portion of the courthouse building is now dedicated to the circuit court.

St. Louis County

Organized: October 1, 1812 | County Seat: Clayton | Architect: Murphy, Downey, Wofford, and Richman

In 1813, the Missouri Territorial Legislature laid out the boundaries of St. Louis County and established the county as one of the territory's first five counties. Early county courts made use of available sites for meetings.

When statehood was achieved in 1821, the legislature appointed commissioners and agreed to appropriate funds for construction of the courthouse. The commissioners accepted land donated by Auguste Chouteau and J. B. C. Lucas, and in 1825, they made an initial appropriation of seven thousand dollars for construction of a courthouse building. A second appropriation of eight thousand dollars followed in 1826, and construction began on the county's first courthouse. The sixty-foot-square building, designed by George Morton and Joseph Laveille, featured a curved portico with rounded steps and a cupola. It was completed four years later.

The need for a larger facility prompted the court to call for a replacement courthouse. Construction started in 1839, and after a series of adaptations and alterations, the St. Louis Courthouse in downtown St. Louis achieved its present appearance in 1862.

In 1876, the City of St. Louis decided to separate from St. Louis County. The downtown St. Louis courthouse ceased to function as the county's courthouse, and the county seat was relocated west of the city of St. Louis. The downtown courthouse was used for municipal purposes until the 1930s, when it was turned over to the United States government and became part of the Jefferson National Expansion Memorial.

Meanwhile, the now independent St. Louis County appointed a courthouse committee and selected a site west of the city in a remote, wooded, undeveloped

Top: Construction on the St. Louis County Government Complex started in 1968, and the complex continued to expand during the twentieth century. The newest addition, the Buzz Westfall Justice Center (left), is a twelve-hundred-bed juvenile detention facility that was completed in 1998. Other structures in the complex include the St. Louis County Courts Building (middle left), the Lawrence C. Roos County Government Building, and the St. Louis County Police Headquarters.

Bottom: This drawing of the original St. Louis County Courthouse is part of the documentation created when the federal government surveyed the building in 1937 as part of the Historic American Buildings Survey—an inventory of the country's most important architecture. (From: Library of Congress)

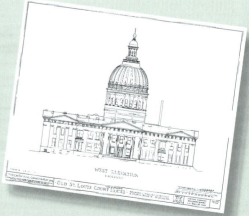

area of land donated by Ralph Clayton and M. F. Hanley. Land was cleared and construction began on St. Louis County's first courthouse that was located outside of the city limits of St. Louis. A cornerstone ceremony for this building was held in 1878. An addition was built in 1912, and that building served the county well into the 1960s.

By the 1960s, St. Louis County was the largest metropolitan area in the state. The government necessary to serve this population was correspondingly large. It was clear that a single courthouse building would no longer suffice, and in 1968, the county built a complex of buildings to house the county's administrative offices, law enforcement, and judicial services. This grouping of county office buildings has become a popular option for many counties in Missouri.

Saline County

Organized: November 25, 1820 | County Seat: Marshall | Architect: John C. Cochrane

During the first twenty years of its existence, the legislature moved the county seat among three different communities—Cambridge, Jonesboro, and Arrow Rock—before settling on Marshall. In 1839, Jeremiah Odell and his wife Elizabeth conveyed sixty-five acres to the county for the purpose of establishing a county seat. The court began meeting there in 1840.

In 1841, the court built the first courthouse in Marshall. It burned during the Civil War. In 1868, a replacement building was erected, but evidentially suffering from poor workmanship or faulty material, it was considered beyond repair less then ten years later and shuttered and closed for good in 1879.

In 1881, voters approved a bond issue to fund the current courthouse. The completed building was accepted by the county in 1882. In 1973, the building was fully restored and still serves as the county courthouse for Saline County. It is listed on the National Register of Historic Places.

Top: The 1882 Saline County Courthouse was refurbished in 1973, and architect Philip Cotton, who planned the restoration, returned the building's trim colors to the original hues of buff, maroon, and blue-green.

Middle: Daniel Boone's sons manufactured salt in Saline County. Their salt-making operations drove off game, disrupted Native American hunting traditions, and unwittingly contributed to the discord that grew between the settlers and Missouri's indigenous people. (From: Missouri State Capitol. Lunette by Victor Higgins)

Bottom left: Odell's signature is on the April 13, 1839, land transfer, but his wife Elizabeth was illiterate and made an "x" mark to indicate her agreement of the contract.

Bottom right: Kenneth R. Bryant, Saline County Clerk, sits beneath a picture of Jeremiah Odell, the man who donated sixty-five acres of land for the county seat in 1839. Bryant is holding a copy of Odell's original transfer of land that sparked creation of the town of Marshall.

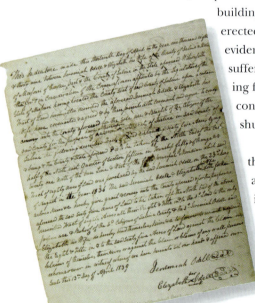

Schuyler County

Organized: February 14, 1845 | County Seat: Lancaster | Architect: Kenneth O. von Achen and Associates

In 1845, Schuyler County's first county seat moved from the town of Tippecannoe to a town a few miles away called Lancaster. There, the court built a small, two-story, frame building as a temporary courthouse. At one point, the court considered painting two sides of this building white and the other two sides red, with green trim on the doors and windows, but the colorful order was rescinded at the next session.

In 1856, the court replaced the temporary building with a neat foursquare-style, two-story, brick building that served the county until 1894. An architect's survey found the building to be unsafe, and it was demolished in preparation for the replacement courthouse, a brick, three-story building with a square tower over the main entrance. That courthouse was replaced by the current courthouse in 1961. The red-brick, white-stone–trimmed building with a modest cupola was a compromise design that was selected after some residents objected to the architect's earlier plan that they judged to be too modern. This building continues to serve as the Schuyler County seat of justice.

Scotland County

Organized: January 29, 1841 | County Seat: Memphis | Architect: W. Chamberlain and Company

The first American settlers to Scotland County's rolling prairie land came in the 1830s, mainly from other Missouri counties and Kentucky and Tennessee. The open rolling prairie land appealed to farmers who were tired of clearing forest land and plowing small acreage farms. The Iowa, Sac, and Fox tribes ceded the land in 1824, but the Sac and Fox were friendly with the pioneer settlers and continued to roam the area until the 1840s. Two well-traveled Indian trails ran north through the county, and more than fifty prehistoric burial mounds remain in the vicinity. A few buffalo still wandered through the tall grass county, and settlers plowed up mastodon bones on land that was later to become the town of Memphis.

In 1841, Scotland County included the land that is now Knox County. In 1843, the legislature divided the territory in half and shifted the county seat from Sand Hill to Memphis, the geographic center of the newly abbreviated county.

In 1844, the community constructed the first courthouse in Memphis. This building was razed in 1857 to make way for the replacement building. The county's second courthouse served until 1905.

Voters authorized construction of the present courthouse the first time the issue was placed on the ballot. This was a rare occurrence and a point of pride in an era when it was common for courthouse bond issues to go before voters numerous times before one was accepted. A cornerstone ceremony was held in October 1907, and the county accepted the building in July 1908. This courthouse still serves as the county's seat of justice.

Top: County Commissioners Win Hill (left), Mike Stephenson, and Paul Campbell listen attentively as Betty Lodewegen, county clerk, discusses an item on the court's agenda.

Bottom: The 1907 Scotland County Courthouse Building Committee selected a stone veneer for the facade of the building instead of brick. The addition of stone cost an extra $2,300.

Scott County

Organized: December 28, 1821 | County Seat: Benton | Architect: Henry H. Hohenschild

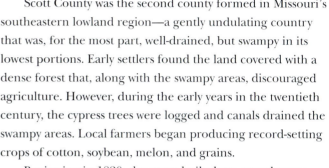

Scott County was the second county formed in Missouri's southeastern lowland region—a gently undulating country that was, for the most part, well-drained, but swampy in its lowest portions. Early settlers found the land covered with a dense forest that, along with the swampy areas, discouraged agriculture. However, during the early years in the twentieth century, the cypress trees were logged and canals drained the swampy areas. Local farmers began producing record-setting crops of cotton, soybean, melon, and grains.

Beginning in 1820, the court built three courthouses in rapid succession in Benton before the outbreak of the Civil War, but each proved to be inadequate or poorly constructed. The first court building was a log structure; the second, in 1844, was built with bricks; and the third, in 1855, was a frame construction.

In 1863, when raids by armed rebels threatened to destroy Benton, officials moved the county seat to Commerce, a town about ten miles east of Benton on the Mississippi River. The people of Commerce built a plain, substantial courthouse building, but by 1878, the town's location proved to be inconvenient and the people voted to move the county seat back to the more centrally located site at Benton.

In 1883, the county constructed its fifth courthouse in Benton. By 1911, the building's shortcomings were well known, and rather than renovate the building, the county officials decided to construct a new courthouse. The building was razed in 1912 to make way for the current courthouse. The court used fifty thousand dollars from general revenue funds to build the courthouse instead of asking voters to pass a bond issue, but in 1912, a forty thousand dollar bond issue was placed before the citizens to pay for finish work on the interior of the building. The levy passed and the building was completed in December 1913. It continues to function as the seat of justice for Scott County. On January 28, 2004, the courthouse was added to the National Register of Historic Places.

Top: To bolster support for passage of a forty thousand dollar bond election needed to finish construction of the 1912 Scott County Courthouse, proponents sponsored a five-hundred-words-or-less essay contest for young people under twenty-one. The first prize of ten dollars was awarded, and the county residents passed the bond issue the following week.

Middle: Scott County Commissioner Jamie Burger played a key role in directing a recent restoration of the courthouse. His wife's great uncle painted the portrait of the courthouse that hangs in the commissioners' chamber. The wall thermostat is original equipment. Scott County has a long and well-deserved reputation for the quality upkeep of its seat of justice. (From: Scott County Collection. Artist: Gregory LeGrand 1975)

Bottom: The well-appointed, vaulted-ceiling courtroom features bulls-eye windows and has been the hall of justice in the Scott County for nearly ninety-five years.

In 1939, the WPA rejected Shannon County's plan for a new courthouse, but the architect scrambled to help the court submit a revised design. The changes were approved.

Shannon County

Organized: January 29, 1841 | County Seat: Eminence | Architect: Dan R. Sanford

Shannon County's territory encompassed a larger geographic area when the legislature authorized its formation in 1841. Three counties—Texas, Reynolds, and Carter—acquired portions of their land area from Shannon when they were organized as individual counties. Eminence, Shannon's county seat, was originally located about ten miles north of its present location, near Round Spring—a limestone spring that discharges an average of thirty-three million gallons of water per day into the scenic Current River. The county's first courthouse, a 16-by-20-foot, hewn-log structure, was built on that site in 1845, but fire caused by a marauding guerrilla band destroyed the building and the town of Eminence during the Civil War. The county's records were lost during this period of devastation.

After the war in 1868, county officials laid out a new town of Eminence in its present location on the Jack's Fork of the Current River. The first courthouse on this site was built in 1868, but it was destroyed by fire in 1871. A replacement courthouse was built but soon became too small for county business, and the county clerk and circuit clerk moved their offices to different buildings on the square. An arsonist burned the courthouse and the clerks' offices in 1895. The courthouse was not severely damaged, but all county records were lost for the second time.

Architect Henry H. Hohenschild designed the replacement courthouse. The plans had to be redrawn in order to bring the cost of the building into line with the $5,000 figure that the county had budgeted for the project. Even with the reduction, space in the courthouse attic was rented to the Odd Fellows for lodge meetings so they might help fund the new building. This building was completed in 1899, but it, too, was destroyed by fire in 1938.

COURT HOUSE, EMINENCE, MO.

The current courthouse, a Work Projects Administration building, was approved for funding in 1939 after initially being rejected by the WPA. Architect Dan R. Sanford helped the court resubmit a revised plan, and the WPA agreed to fund $52,000. The county financed the remaining $25,500. The building was completed in the summer of 1941. This court-house continues to serve the people of Shannon County.

Top: Rare postcards of courthouses are highly prized by collectors. This postcard of the 1899–1938 Shannon County Courthouse was purchased on an Internet auction site. (From: postcard, Melany Williams collection)

Bottom: George Shannon, for whom Shannon County was named, was the youngest member of the Lewis and Clark Expedition. Shannon lost a leg, and nearly his life, during a return trip up the Missouri River but lived to write of his adventures, become a successful lawyer, and befriend Henry Clay and other powerful political leaders of the age. He died in 1836 while attending to legal business in Marion County and is buried one mile north of Palmyra.

GEORGE SHANNON

1787-1836

THIS MARKER COMMEMORATES GEORGE SHANNON, THE YOUNGEST MEMBER OF THE CORPS OF DISCOVERY, ON THE OCCASION OF THE BICENTENNIAL OF THE LEWIS AND CLARK EXPEDITION.

HE DIED IN PALMYRA, MISSOURI WHILE ON LEGAL BUSINESS, AUGUST 30, 1836, AND IS BURIED ONE MILE NORTH OF PALMYRA IN THE MASSEY MILL CEMETERY.

MARKER DEDICATED ON JUNE 13, 2004 BY THE MISSOURI STATE SOCIETY DAR AND THE HANNIBAL HERITAGE CHAPTER, DAR

Shelby County

Organized: January 2, 1835 | County Seat: Shelbyville | Architect: Jerome B. Legg

The first railroads entered Missouri in the 1850s and altered the state's transportation routes. Rivers meandered, but railroads were constructed on right-of-ways that were built to be as straight as possible. Missouri's northern tier of counties provided the open prairie that fledgling railroad companies desired. River routes began to lose favor as railroads connected Omaha and Kansas City with the rapidly ascending city of Chicago and other markets in the east.

The Hannibal and St. Joseph Railroad Association was formed in 1846 in the Hannibal office of lawyer John Clemens, father of then eleven-year-old Sam Clemens, who dreamt of becoming a riverboat pilot. The Association was formed to raise money to link the east and west ends of the state over the most direct route. Several Missouri counties helped finance railroads by selling bonds, but the rampant cost overruns caused many bankruptcies and these ventures were highly speculative—similar to the "dot-com" boom and bust of the twentieth century.

Despite setbacks, Missouri's east-west railroad was completed in 1859. In 1857, the rail line had reached southern Shelby County. Shelbyville, the county seat, had to utilize a spur line to connect with the railhead in Shelbina.

In 1837, Shelbyville's first courthouse was a foursquare building that was expanded in 1878 with the addition of wings at the front corners of the main building. A fire that started in the cupola destroyed the courthouse in 1891.

Voters promptly approved the funds for construction of a replacement courthouse in September 1891, only a few months after the fire. However, actual progress was slow and the completion date was almost a year past the projected date. The court subtracted $580 from the final payment to the contractor because of damage that was caused by delays in construction. The county accepted the building in July 1893. In 1909, workers added plumbing and steam heat to the courthouse. Other renovations, such as installing hard wood floors on the first floor, were made to the building during the following decades.

Top: In 1929, Shelby County printed coupons for bonds to raise funds for construction of a railroad line between Shelbyville and Shelbina.

Middle: The 1891 Shelby County Courthouse has three entrances—south, east, and west. One resident was convinced that major growth was destined to occur on the north side of the square and became incensed when the court did not change the plans and install a fourth entrance on the north side of the building.

Bottom: One headline bemoaned the destruction of the "beautiful" courthouse, but other reports were less kind and insinuated that the loss of the building was for the best due to its poor conditions and unsuitability for county functions. (From: *Shelby County Herald*, August 7, 1985, Early History edition)

Stoddard County

Organized: January 2, 1835 | County Seat: Bloomfield | Architect: Unknown; P. H. Weathers (1909 remodeling)

In 1835, the court built Stoddard County's first courthouse—a small, two-story, brick building. This building served the community for twenty years. In 1856, it was replaced by a larger, two-story, brick, almost-square building. The building was destroyed during General Price's 1864 Civil War raid that was stopped at the Battle of Pilot Knob in Iron County.

In 1861, during the Civil War, Union soldiers briefly occupied Bloomfield and printed the first edition of the *Stars and Stripes*, a newspaper for soldiers. Troopers with printing expertise commandeered a newspaper office across the square from the courthouse and quickly ran copies of a one-page newspaper. Only four editions of the *Stars and Stripes* were printed during the Civil War, and the newspaper was all but forgotten after the war. General Pershing, a Missouri native, authorized a military newspaper for his troops during World War I, and the name was resurrected as the army's official military newspaper. The newspaper was revived again during World War II and continues to be published for American forces stationed around the world.

Top: Remodeled in 1909, the present Stoddard County Courthouse is an expansion and renovation of a core building that was built in 1867.

Middle: Stoddard County Clerk Don White generally has a ready smile and some good fishing stories to tell, but his jovial mood was diverted as he tracked tornados on his computer that were reported to be touching down near Stoddard County's southern border late one afternoon in the spring of 2006. Fortunately, only minor damage was reported.

Bottom: The military newspaper *Stars and Stripes* got its start in a newspaper office about fifty feet from the front steps of the Stoddard County Courthouse.

In 1867, the community built a new courthouse. It was a square, brick building with a pointed spire rising from a square base on the roof. Work on the building was completed in 1870, and this structure provided the core building for a major remodeling that took place in 1909. Architect P. H. Weathers's design included reinforcing the foundations, adding new brick wings, covering the outer walls with a brick veneer, and replacing the spire with a central tower. The remodeled 1867 Stoddard County Courthouse continues to serve the citizens of the county.

Stone County

Organized: February 10, 1851 | County Seat: Galena | Architect: Charles Sudoelter and Company

In 1852, the court met for the first time in the town of Jamestown. Early the next year, county officials decided to change the name of the town to Galena—the metallurgical name for lead ore. Also in 1853, the court sold public land to raise funds and authorized $376 for the construction of a two-story, hewn-log courthouse.

Over the next two decades, county officials continued to use this building, but despite painting it in 1854 and repairing its foundation and chimney in 1858, the building fell into poor condition. In 1867, the courthouse was in such a dilapidated state that the county clerk moved his office to a private residence located a few yards from the courthouse. In 1870, the court ordered the construction of a replacement courthouse for the county, but progress was slow and four years passed before the court accepted the building.

Once again, the courthouse fell into poor condition, and by 1919, only three offices remained in the building; the county's other offices were spread to different locations around the square. In 1919, this building was razed to make way for Stone County's twentieth-century courthouse.

The county's present courthouse was completed in 1920. The eighty-six-year-old building remains in service. In 1998, the county moved its law enforcement and justice operations to a new judicial center located near the east side of the square.

Top: Exterior stairs provided access to the offices on the second floor of the 1870–1919 Stone County Courthouse. Judges preferred exterior staircases because foot traffic on an interior flight of steps caused noise and disrupted court proceedings. (From: Stone County Collection. Artist R. Kuhl, 1990)

Bottom: The 1920 Stone County Courthouse remains true to it original design. A nearby 1998 judicial center now houses the county's law enforcement and court operations.

Sullivan County

Organized: February 14, 1845 | County Seat: Milan | Architect: Lyle V. DeWitt

Top: The 1939 Sullivan County Courthouse was designed by Lyle V. DeWitt, a young, 23-year-old architect and native of the county. DeWitt foresaw the need for elevators in the building at some future date and included shafts for them in his plans.

Middle: Nellie Dixon (left), juvenile officer, and Jackie Morris, deputy county clerk, check on the stock in a food pantry that operates from the courthouse's community room. The pantry, staffed by volunteers, has been a feature at the courthouse for the last twenty years.

Bottom: Bill Littrell, a retired schoolteacher, waits in the lobby of the Sullivan County Courthouse for his first client to appear. Littrell works for the Ninth Circuit's Drug Court and regularly meets with offenders on an individual basis to monitor their progress.

In 1846, the Sullivan County court ordered eight hundred dollars worth of brick for the construction of its first courthouse in Milan. The following year, it rescinded its plans and instead built a modest one-story, hewn-log building. The supply of bricks was quietly stockpiled.

The land that became the county square had formerly contained an odd, V-shaped earthen mound that pointed northwest and reached a height of fifteen feet at the highest point. While leveling the mound, workmen uncovered the remains of three Native Americans with stones placed around the skeletons. The stones from the burial mound were used to build the foundation for the new jail.

In 1857, the hoard of bricks was used to build the county's second courthouse. By 1891, however, the building was in poor condition and in need of replacement. Repair of the roof and interior helped maintain the building for a few more years, but it was razed after a fire in 1908.

The court officials used an insurance payment of six thousand dollars to purchase temporary quarters—a former railroad company building. This temporary courthouse building was used for the next thirty years.

In 1938, the county built a new courthouse using financial assistance provided by the Work Projects Administration. This courthouse continues to serve the people of Sullivan County.

Taney County

Organized: January 6, 1837 | County Seat: Forsyth | Architect: Volney A. Poulson (1951) and Hood-Rich Inc. (1990 Remodel)

In 1837, the court met in private homes while a courthouse site was being selected in Forsyth. Before a permanent structure could be built in that community, however, the state legislature appointed commissioners who decided to relocate the county seat to a site near Bull Creek. This impulsive move annoyed the citizens of Forsyth, and they vigorously lobbied the legislature until the county seat was returned to Forsyth in 1845.

Around 1855, the community constructed a three-story courthouse, which was considered a rare structure for this period. This building was severely damaged on July 22, 1861, during a Civil War battle. Following the war, the building was either repaired or a new building was built. The record is unclear as to which took place. In either case, a fire destroyed the building on December 19, 1885.

A replacement courthouse was completed in 1891, but when Bull Shoals Lake inundated the area in 1951, the courthouse had to be abandoned. This was the third Missouri courthouse to be flooded by the construction of a man-made lake. Before the waters covered the building, the county sold it to the School of the Ozarks (renamed College of the Ozarks or "Hard Work U"). The building was dismantled, and its stones were used to build a campus building in 1952.

The county selected higher ground to build its present courthouse. This courthouse, occupied on August 1, 1952, reflected architect Volney A. Poulson's unique interest in Southwestern design. He designed a one-story, stucco-covered, 116-square-foot building that enclosed a 42-foot-square, open-air courtyard.

Top: The Taney County Courthouse after its 1990 remodeling.

Middle left: Taney County Collector Sheila Wyatt notes that she deposits the county's cash in a nearby federally insured depository despite the fact that her office is equipped with a formidable safe.

Middle right: This document is a 1913 Certification of Ordination filed with the county clerk confirming that the Rev. George A. Roberts was authorized to preach the gospel and administer the ordinances by the General Baptist denomination in Taney County, or wherever God might call him. The board, slipped between the bound pages of record books, provides a hard surface for hand written entries.

Bottom: An architect's rendering in the courthouse lobby, coupled with the passage of a sales tax that went into effect in April 2006, indicates that a new justice center annex and remodeling of the courthouse may be in the Taney County's immediate future.

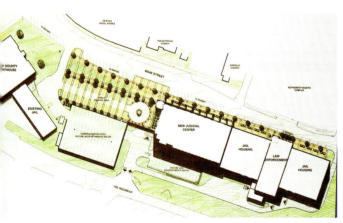

In 1990, Hood-Rich Inc., a Springfield architectural and engineering firm, extensively remodeled the building. A second floor was added and a tower was placed over the main entrance. The open courtyard was enclosed and used for office space. The renovations were completed in 1991. This building remains in service as the Taney County Courthouse.

Top: The initial plans for the 1932 Texas County Courthouse differed from what was actually built. The architect envisioned a native stone building with a brick face and terra cotta trim. However, financial pressure, exacerbated by the Depression, dictated a simpler design that utilized the foundation of the old courthouse.

Bottom: Tammy Cantrell, Texas County Treasurer and Ex Officio Collector, commissioned a patriotic theme for a mural in the treasurer's office. (From: Texas County Collection. Artist: Steven Allen Sewell, 2005)

Texas County

Organized: February 14, 1845 | County Seat: Houston | Architect: E. S. Johnson

Texas County was originally known as Ashley County, but its name was changed when the county was formally chartered by the state legislature in 1845 and named in honor of the annexation of the Republic of Texas by the United States (a move that triggered the outbreak of the Mexican-American War in 1846). The county is Missouri's largest in terms of geographic size, and it is one of the few counties in the United States that borders eight other counties.

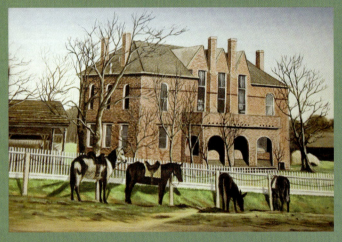

The governor had to appoint three different sets of commissioners before the final group acted by selecting eighty acres to be set aside as a site for the county seat. In keeping with the Texas connection, the commissioners named the seat Houston.

The county seat was destroyed twice during the Civil War, and by war's end, the town was empty of all inhabitants. Until people slowly began to re-populate Houston, some court sessions were held in the town of Licking.

The first courthouse built after the Civil War was a 44-foot-square, two-story building. Construction of the building, along with landscaping and fencing the perimeter, was completed in 1871. In 1881, fire damaged that building, and the court ordered a similar structure erected on the foundation of the old building. That building was completed in 1882.

Top: The 1881 Texas County Courthouse before its 1901 alteration. (From: Texas County Collection)

Bottom: The 1881 Texas County Courthouse after it was remodeled in 1901. Architect Henry H. Hohenschild drew plans for the extensive remodeling project. (From: Texas County Collection. Artist Kay Adams)

In 1901, extensive alterations were made to the building, increasing its size and transforming it into a rectangular structure with a triple-arched, one-story portico over the entrance. Fire destroyed the building in 1930. Building the replacement courthouse, however, would prove to be a burden for the county.

The 1929 stock market collapse and the depression that followed spread fear throughout the nation. The hard-pressed citizens of Texas County clearly indicated they had no intention of voting for more indebtedness, and in 1931, the court avoided almost certain defeat at the ballot box by canceling a proposed courthouse bond issue election. The court decided instead to clear away the foundation and rebuild using the insurance money they had received from the fire. Those funds were not sufficient to complete the task, however. and in September 1931, the voters did agree to a modest bond issue in order to finish construction on the building. The brick and stone courthouse was completed in 1932 and continues to serve the people of Texas County.

Vernon County

Organized: February 27, 1855 | County Seat: Nevada | Architect: Robert G. Kirsch

The border warfare that raged between Missouri and Kansas during the Civil War led to the destruction in 1863 of the county's 1856 courthouse and an 1860 county clerk's office building. The county seat was moved from Nevada to avoid further devastation to that community, and the county's pre-war records were hidden in Arkansas and Kansas but were returned after the war. However, court records from 1861–65 were lost.

After the war, a replacement building was erected in 1868 and served the county for nearly forty years. In 1906, county officials found the building beyond repair and sold it to make way for a replacement courthouse.

In 1906, the court appointed a building committee of twenty citizens to make recommendations for a replacement courthouse. The committee reviewed plans from ten different courthouse architects and, with a tower clock donation already in hand, recommended that the court use the plans submitted by the well-known and prolific courthouse architect, Robert G. Kirsch.

Work began in 1906. The county accepted the completed building in 1908. The still hard-at-work Vernon County Courthouse was added to the National Register of Historic Places on June 27, 1997.

Top: Bids exceeded the seventy-five thousand dollars that the court had budgeted for the project, so Architect Kirsch modified his design to reduce expenses. Final costs amounted to about eighty thousand dollars.

Middle and bottom: David Darnold, Vernon County Presiding Commissioner, checks the minutes of the county court's most recent meeting before posting the report on the county's website. Computers and Internet connections permit greater access to county information by the public and speed communications between local, state, and federal agencies.

Bottom far right: In 1906, the court recognized that building a courthouse can be a rancorous process, and they chose a committee with twenty members to air diverse opinions and ensure consensus for the selected design.

Warren County

Organized: January 5, 1833 | County Seat: Warrenton | Architects: Phillips Swager Associates, H. Daniel Willett (project architect)

Few county boundaries remained unchanged during the days when the State Legislature was dividing larger counties into smaller units. In 1833, for example, Warren County was divided from Montgomery County. In 1818, Montgomery County had been divided from St. Charles County, which had been created in 1812. And, even though all of Missouri's 114 counties were created by 1861, adjustments to the borders of many of the counties continued into the 1870s.

In 1836, after three years of considering various sites, the voters approved Warrenton as the county seat. Early court sessions there were held in private homes while construction of a courthouse began in 1837. The county's first courthouse was completed the next year, and it served as the seat of justice until 1871, when it was sold at auction and later razed. The court had begun work on a replacement courthouse in 1869, and it was ready of occupancy in 1871. In 1972, that building was placed on the National Register of Historic Places but has since been demolished. The cupola and some of the foundation stones are on display at the Warren County Historical Society Museum and Historical Library, located across the street from the county square and the replacement courthouse.

In 1995, work began on the county's present courthouse. It was occupied in 1997 and a dedication ceremony was held in 1998. General contractor on the project was Demien Construction, Wentzville, Missouri.

Top: Warren County's 1995 courthouse was designed by Phillips Swager Associates, with H. Daniel Willett serving as project architect. Damien Construction served as contractor.

Middle: Road and bridge maintenance is one of the county commission's responsibilities. Warren County Commissioners Arden Engelage (left), Fred Vahle, and Jim Logan listen to a presentation from Richard Kathriner and Ron Holt of Thompson Culvert Company.

Bottom: The cupola and foundation stones from 1870–1995 Warren County Courthouse are on display at the Warren County Historical Society's museum and historical library.

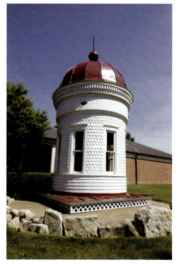

Washington County

Organized: August 21, 1813 |
County Seat: Potosi | Architect:
Henry H. Hohenschild

Top: The 1907 Washington County Courthouse was constructed for a cost of about thirty thousand dollars and is similar in design to the neighboring Madison County Courthouse that was designed by Theodore C. Link.

Bottom: The 1849–1907 Washington County Courthouse was reputedly set ablaze by a cigar-toting pigeon that carried a still-lit stogie back to her nest in the building's eves overhang. The building had been remodeled ten years earlier. (From: Washington County Collection)

In 1833, the county commissioners selected Mine a Breton—a mining village that was later renamed Potosi—as Washington County's county seat. Moses Austin and his partner, John Rice Jones, donated fifty acres of land as the site for the county seat.

In 1814, the court began construction on Washington County's first courthouse.

In 1849, that building was razed and some of the material recycled for use in building the next courthouse.

The replacement courthouse was completed in 1850 and survived a Civil War cannon bombardment. It burned in 1906. The present courthouse was constructed in 1907 on the same site. It escaped being destroyed by fire in 2002 because of a fish tank.

An overloaded electric receptacle sparked a fire in the prosecuting attorney's office. The heat became so intense that it shattered a large fish tank on a nearby table. The water from the tank doused the flames, leaving a smoldering rug that produced copious smoke. The smoke billowed from the building and alerted the community before the fire could do more damage.

The courthouse remains in service, and some wags now say it is all right for things to be a little "fishy" in the courthouse.

Village de la mine à Breton

Opposite page: Moses Austin helped establish Mine a Breton, a mining community that was later renamed Potosi, as the county seat of Washington County. This map shows the boundaries and location of Austin's land concession granted by the Spanish colonial government. (From: Missouri State Archives)

This page: The 1940 Wayne County Courthouse was funded by the seventy thousand dollars that the federal government paid the county as compensation for submerging their former courthouse. The county received a WPA grant to fund the remaining cost of the ninety-eight thousand dollar construction project.

Wayne County

Organized: December 11, 1818 | County Seat: Greenville | Architects: Eugene S. Johnson and Albert C. Maack

Wayne County, one of Missouri's earliest established counties, constructed five courthouses before becoming the second county forced to construct a courthouse on higher ground in 1940 to avoid the rising waters of a man-made lake, Lake Wappapello. Camden County had a similar experience in 1930 when the Lake of the Ozarks inundated Linn Creek.

In anticipation of the rising waters, the federal government condemned Wayne County's courthouse, a building that was only twelve years old. Federal compensation and a Work Projects Administration grant were bundled to fund the construction of a replacement courthouse on higher ground. Construction of the Wappapello Dam was started in September 1938 and was completed in June 1941. As predicted, the lake inundated the historic town of Greenville.

Along with the excitement and commotion that accompanied the lake's creation, two contending communities—Patterson and Piedmont—challenged Greenville for the honor of being the county seat. After several countywide elections, Greenville remained the people's choice. Once that issue was settled, construction work began in 1941 on a new courthouse. The building was completed in 1943. The three-story building continues to serve the county.

Webster County

Organized: March 3, 1855 | County Seat: Marshfield | Architect: Earl Hawkins

In 1855, the state legislature formed Webster County from parts of Greene, Dallas, Christian, and Wright Counties. Marshfield, the Webster County Seat, claims the highest elevation of any county seat in Missouri. It is located at thirteen hundred feet above sea level on the high plateau of the Ozark Mountains.

In 1857, the court occupied Webster County's first courthouse, a rectangular frame building. That building was destroyed six years later during a Civil War incident. After the war, a replacement courthouse was authorized in 1868 and completed in 1870. This was a large, two-story, brick courthouse. In 1880, that building was a place of safety for townspeople when a tornado demolished Marshfield and tragically killed eighty-seven people who were not able to reach shelter in time.

The courthouse was damaged by the tornado. The court ordered repairs to be made that same year and authorized the addition of a cupola over the main entry. Many complaints about the poor quality of the building were registered in the years that followed, but it was not until fifty years later, in 1930, that an engineering firm officially documented the deplorable condition of the building. The Springfield firm's report was such a dire warning that several clerks' offices and the county court evacuated the building, and the second floor courtroom was closed. However, it was not ordered closed and razed until 1939, when the replacement courthouse was ready to be occupied.

This view of the 1939 Webster County Courthouse includes the scale model of NASA's Hubble Telescope, named in honor of Webster County's native son, Edwin Hubble. Among his many contributions to the world of astronomy, Hubble proved that the universe is expanding.

Voters authorized a bond issue for the present courthouse in 1938, and after the Work Projects Administration accepted the proposed plan for a new building and agreed to help fund the construction, work began in 1939. Cost of the building amounted to about one hundred and fifty thousand dollars, and construction was completed in 1941.

The 1898 Worth County Courthouse came dangerously close to being condemned after being closed in 1980, but the community rallied to restore the old building and provide regular maintenance.

Worth County

Organized: February 8, 1861 | County Seat: Grant City | Architects: Fremont C. Orff and Ernest F. Guilbert

Missouri was admitted into the Union as a state in 1821 with a population of about 67,000 settlers who resided in a handful of established counties located on or near either the Mississippi or Missouri Rivers. Within forty years, the population had increased to 1,182,012, and people had spread to all corners of the state, requiring a growth in the number of counties until the state legislature authorized the 114th and final county on February 8, 1861. That last county was Worth County, and its formation completed the modern map of the bootheel state.

Worth County's first county seat was established in 1861 in Smithton, but within two years, residents of the county petitioned for the county seat to be moved to Grant City, which was a more central location. The court built its first courthouse in Grant City in 1863, but three years later that building was destroyed by fire. A replacement courthouse was ordered the same year, and one thousand dollars was appropriated to construct a frame, two-story building that measured 40 by 32 feet.

By 1882, the dark, dirty, and poorly ventilated courthouse was considered unacceptable as a seat of justice, but fifteen years would pass before the court could garner public support for a new courthouse. In 1897, the voters passed a twenty-five thousand dollar bond issue for a new courthouse, and architects Fremont C. Orff and Ernest F. Guilbert, of Minneapolis, submitted the winning design. Construction was completed in February 1899, and officials soon after occupied their new offices.

The following years took their toll, and the building's condition deteriorated through lack of preventive maintenance and regular upkeep. In 1980, the courthouse had to be closed because of its poor condition; the courthouse was clearly in crisis.

In December 1981, the Worth County Commissioners established the Worth County Courthouse Betterment Association and appointed J. O. Lynch and Ed McLeod to co-chair the committee. Their group raised approximately fifty thousand dollars to restore the building that was showing every one of its eighty-three years. Repair work included new windows and metal doors, painting, guttering, roofing, and other restorative work. In 1984, impressed by the revival of the building, Worth County voters approved a levy for the on-going maintenance of the courthouse, such as tuck pointing in 1998.

The courthouse was closed for a second time in 2000—albeit temporarily—for roof repair work. The now 108-year-old building received a new lease on life and continues to serve Worth County.

Top: Citizens gathered on the courthouse lawn on Memorial Day in 1915 to commemorate the fallen soldiers of the Civil War—a conflict that had ended only fifty years before. Speeches at the courthouse were common occurrences in the days before radio and television delivered news and events over the airwaves. (From: Worth County Collection)

Bottom: Firewood stacked in the snow confirms the fact that nineteenth century public buildings, such as this 1866–97 Worth County Courthouse, were heated by fireplaces and iron stoves. Light was provided by windows or lanterns, and few buildings of the period offered the luxury of indoor plumbing. (From: Worth County Collection)

Historical artifacts are preserved at the Wright County Historical and Genealogical Society headquarters and museum, located across the square from the courthouse in Hartville. Anne Truster (left), volunteer, and Phyllis Rippee, office supervisor, welcome visitors to the society's museum and gladly answer questions about life and times in Wright County. These women personify the unflagging hospitality and dedication to local history and preservation that is typical of Missouri's county historical societies.

Wright County

Organized: January 29, 1841 | County Seat: Hartsville | Architect: Roger Frangkiser

Top: The 1898–1964 Wright County Courthouse made a handsome picture postcard, but its soft-fired exterior created maintenance problems for the county. (From: Wright County Historical & Genealogical Society Collection)

Bottom: The Wright County Library occupies the one-story annex (far left) of the 1964 Wright County Courthouse. Construction costs for the modern-design building were about $280,000.

In 1898, the county court ordered construction of a new building to replace its Civil War era courthouse that had been damaged the year before by a tornado. However, the new courthouse caused many maintenance frustrations during the next sixty-five years because its exterior was finished with soft brick.

Hard-fired, or face brick, is fired at a higher temperature to produce a surface on the brick that resists weathering; but soft-fired, or common brick, is subject to rotting and crumbling when exposed to the elements. Hard-fired brick is usually used for building exteriors, and soft-fired brick is reserved for interior walls.

The 1898 courthouse was demolished in January 1964 while the current courthouse was being constructed. In 1962, county officials had learned of new government funds available to help build public buildings. The courthouse's dilapidated condition made Wright County a likely recipient, and the county applied for a grant.

Under the Accelerated Public Works Program, the Community Facilities Administration provided a $187,000 grant in July 1963, and Wright County citizens approved a matching $187,000 in August 1963. The construction contract was awarded in November 1963, and the present courthouse was opened for county business in January 1965.

State Helps Counties Preserve Rare Documents

Licenses, deeds, wills, contracts, minutes, records, letters, reports, and many other bits and pieces of history come to rest in the vault of a county courthouse. Many of those files are meant to be retained forever. County officials consider all of the records to be important, but some are one-of-a-kind documents, such as Daniel Boone's 1798 Spanish land concession. Other records, such as court reports and deeds, are plentiful but gain historical significance because of the fame of a person associated with them. Examples include the not guilty verdict from the outlaw Frank James' 1883 murder trial in Daviess County and Dred Scott's original 1846 petition for emancipation in St. Louis County.

The Missouri Secretary of State implemented the Local Records Preservation Program in 1986 as a pilot program to help manage and safeguard important records generated on the local level. In 1990, the General Assembly authorized a full-time program to service the needs of local government and Missouri citizens. The program is funded by a one-dollar user fee collected by the recorder of deeds on filings of permanent records. Program resources are recycled back to local governments. The department is housed at the James Kirkpatrick Information Center in Jefferson City.

A vital component of the Local Records Preservation Program is the work conducted on-site throughout the state by field archivists. Archivists aid local officials in records management and preservation maintenance needs by determining the contents of their holdings, identifying what may be discarded, and preparing a computer-generated inventory.

The conservation aspect of the Local Records Preservation Program has been in operation since 1991. Conservators examine, house, and treat documents, maps, and photographs held by local government officials. Large-format and black-and-white duplicates of materials can be made for preservation and security. Conservators are available for site and collections surveys and evaluations identifying areas of need. This information is helpful when applying for grants. The conservation staff consults on display, disaster preparedness, environmental control, preservation housing, shelving and storage, pest management, in-house training, and other preservation issues.

Courthouse officials handle thousands of records every year, and they are vigilant when it comes to protecting and preserving those documents. Many counties now routinely scan their paper documents to produce permanent digital copies and work closely with the state archivists and preservation experts to identify and preserve their irreplaceable files for posterity.

Opposite page

Clockwise from top left:
The Local Records Department is located at the James Kirkpatrick Information Center in Jefferson City.

Sandy Hempe, preservation specialist, joined the lab in 1991 soon after the local records preservation program began. The restoration process for a document usually begins by painstakingly erasing grime one small section at a time.

Repeated soakings help loosen old glue and tape used on the document during earlier attempts to repair the sheet. Modern restoration experts are careful to make repairs that can be removed by future preservationists without damaging the paper.

Torn spots are patched with a covering of acid-free paper and special glue that can be easily removed by future preservationists should the need arise. Even small flakes from brittle documents are saved and glued back into place.

Documents are placed between sheets of matte paper that have been soaked in specially distilled water. The damp blotter sheets loosen any chemicals and minerals. This process is repeated numerous times to gradually wash away stains and grime.

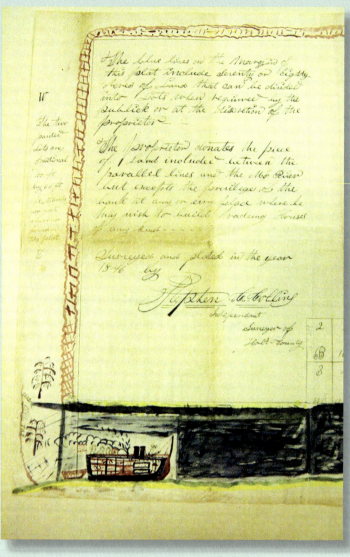

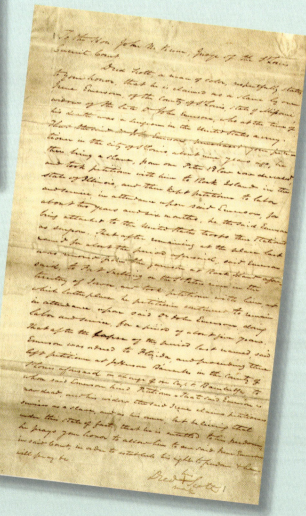

Top: When cleaning a document, a preservationist has to know what to remove and what to leave in place. This ink sketch of riverboat was added to a plat record during the nineteenth century by an anonymous clerk. It is as much a part of the historical document as the property boundary lines.

Bottom: Dred Scott's 1846 petition to sue for freedom was granted in St. Louis County, but the decision was appealed and, in 1857, denied by the United States Supreme Court. (Courtesy: State Archives)

Top: Robert A. Dixon, Recorder of Deeds for Taney County, is a satisfied client of the Document Conservation Lab. The county's plat records were cleaned and now hang in folders to protect them from wear and contamination. Documents sent to the lab for restoration are copied for backup in case the original is lost.

Bottom: In 1798, Spanish authorities awarded Daniel Boone 1,000 arpents (about 850 acres) to settle in Missouri plus 600 arpents for every family he brought with him. Boone and his son Daniel Morgan settled their families in the Femme Osage District, near present day Defiance. (Courtesy: State Archives)

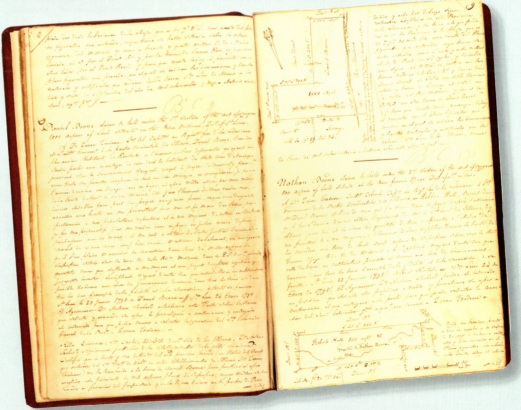

Bibliography

Borneman, Walter R. *1812: The War that Forged a Nation.* New York: HarperCollins Publishers, 2004.

Burnett, Robyn, and Ken Luebbering. *German Settlement in Missouri: New Land, Old Ways.* Columbia, MO: University of Missouri Press, 1996.

Christensen, Lawrence O., William E. Foley, Gary R. Kremer, and Kenneth H. Winn, eds. *Dictionary of Missouri Biography.* Columbia, MO: University of Missouri Press, 1999.

Dufur, Brett, et al. *Lewis and Clark's Journey Across Missouri.* Fayette, MO: Missouri Life Inc., 2003.

Filbert, Preston, and Jim Finlay. *St. Joseph News-Press: 150 years of St. Joseph News.* St. Joseph, MO: News-Press & Gazette Company, 1995.

Gilmore, Donald L. *Civil War on the Missouri–Kansas Border.* Gretna, LA: Pelican Publishing Company, 2006.

Isaacs, Sally S. *America in the Time of Lewis and Clark 1801 to 1850.* Chicago: Heinemann Library, 1998.

Kremer, Gary R., and Antonio F. Holland. *Missouri's Black Heritage.* Revised Edition. Columbia, MO: University of Missouri Press, 1993.

LeSueur, Stephen C. *The 1838 Mormon War in Missouri.* Columbia, MO: University of Missouri Press, 1987.

Loguda-Summers, Debra. "Andrew Taylor Still (1828–1917): The Father of Osteopathic Medicine." Unpublished essay, Still National Osteopathic Museum, Kirksville, MO, 2005.

McCandless, Perry. *A History of Missouri, Volume II: 1820 to 1860.* Columbia, MO: University of Missouri Press, 2000.

McCandless, Perry, and William E. Foley. *Missouri, Then and Now.* Columbia, MO: University of Missouri Press, 2001.

Nagel, Paul C. *Missouri: A History.* Lawrence, KS: University of Kansas Press, 1977.

Ohman, Marian M. *Encyclopedia of Missouri Courthouses.* Columbia, MO: University of Missouri–Columbia Extension Division, 1981.

Ohman, Marion M. *A History of Missouri's Counties, County Seats, and Courthouse Squares.*
Columbia, MO: University of Missouri-Columbia Extension Division, 1983.

Phillips, Charles, and Betty Burnett. *Missouri: Crossroads of the Nation.* Sun Valley, CA: American
Historical Press, 2003.

Wappapello Lake Master Plan. St. Louis District of the U.S. Army Corps of Engineers. Approved
1946, revised 1958, and updated 1963, 1975, and 1985.

Waugh, John C. *On the Brink of Civil War: The Compromise of 1850 and How It Changed the Course of
American History.* Wilmington, DE: Scholarly Resources Inc., 2003.

Wolferman, Kristie C. *The Osage in Missouri.* Columbia, MO: University of Missouri Press, 1997.

About the Author

Dennis Weiser earned a bachelor of journalism from the University of Missouri–Columbia and a master of arts from Lindenwood University at St. Charles. He worked as a photojournalist with the *Rocky Mountain News* in Denver before moving into the world of corporate communica-tion and marketing. During the 1990s, Mr. Weiser served as the executive director for several non-profit organizations. He has taught communication and journalism courses at the college level. Mr. Weiser is a fifth-generation Missourian. His maternal great-grandfather moved to Monroe County from Kentucky and worked as a gandy dancer on the Hannibal-St. Joseph railroad. In the early nineteenth century, his paternal great-great-grandfather migrated from Pennsylvania to trap and fish in southern Buchanan County soon after the 1837 Platte Purchase. Mr. Weiser lives in Jefferson City.